FROM CARDIFF

Edited by Dave Thomas

First published in Great Britain in 2000 by
YOUNG WRITERS
Remus House,
Coltsfoot Drive,
Woodston,
Peterborough, PE2 9JX
Telephone (01733) 890066

All Rights Reserved

Copyright Contributors 1999

HB ISBN 0 75431 780 3
SB ISBN 0 75431 781 1

FOREWORD

This year, the Young Writers' Future Voices competition proudly presents a showcase of the best poetic talent from over 42,000 up-and-coming writers nationwide.

Successful in continuing our aim of promoting writing and creativity in children, our regional anthologies give a vivid insight into the thoughts, emotions and experiences of today's younger generation, displaying their inventive writing in its originality.

The thought, effort, imagination and hard work put into each poem impressed us all and again the task of editing proved challenging due to the quality of entries received, but was nevertheless enjoyable. We hope you are as pleased as we are with the final selection and that you continue to enjoy *Future Voices From Cardiff* for many years to come.

CONTENTS

Glan Ely High School

Laura Taylor	63
Nicola Jones	64
Kelsie Dyer	64
Emma Beech	64
Matthew Stevens	65
Ross Penfold	65
Danielle Cross	66
Katie Wright	66
Hayley Purse	67
Nicola Osman	67

Whitchurch High School

Tyrone Herbert	67
Louise Spinola	68
Tyrone Gharibi	69
Patrick Howell	69
Robert Critchley	70
Christopher Smith	70
Luke Nash	71
Christine James	72
Rhys Heal	72
Estelle Stock	73
Tim Mordecai	74
Rhys Oxenham	74
Jamie-Leigh Deane	75
Rhydian Parry-Owens	75
Donna-Marie Huntley	76
Nadia Refae	76
Fiona Edwards	77
Catherine West	78
Sarah Stinton	78
Rebecca McCrann	79
Lucy Bird	80
Tobias Holmes	80
Joe Tandy	81
Dafydd Salaman	81
Holly Slater	82
Emily Graff	82

Samantha Arnold	83
Christopher Powell	83
Joseph Dodd	84
Carly Jones	84
Carolyn Dugon	85
Jennifer Davidson	86
Antony Goodman	86
Gemma Wilding	87
Rebecca Richards	88
Sarah Francis	89
Laura Miles	90
Daniel Atkinson	91
Gemma Collard	92
Lauren Stacey	93
Charles Moore	93
Samantha Kenealy	94
Kate Holtam	94
Jessica Robson-Davis	95
Rachel Booy	96
Andrew Bridgeman	96
Nia Edwards	97
Martha Kane	97
Andrew Dyson	98
Nicholas Shepherd	98
Rachel Edwards	99
Laura Jones	99
Leon Daly	100
Luke James	100
Matthew Richards	101
Rhiannôn Clarke	101
Samantha James	102
Laura Williams	102
Kyle Smith	103
Matthew Edmonds	103
Laura Diamond	104
Jenny Donoghue	104
Kayleigh Llewellyn	105
Stephanie Bassett	106

The Poems

SWEET SHOP

I walk in the shop with my eyes open wide,
My pocket bulging with money inside,
Pick 'n' mix Smarties, Snickers or Mars,
Oh so many chocolate bars.

Up on the shelves are magazines galore,
Should I buy chocolate or learn some more,
My head is in a turmoil I cannot decide,
To have a Kit-Kat or expand my mind.

Oh no! I see bon-bons and sherbet dips,
Millions, humbugs and sherbet pips.
Oh dear me I just can't think
Never mind I'll buy a *drink!*

Jamie Perkins (11)
Cardiff High School

BROTHER

He's not an alien from outer space,
Only my brother.
He's not a marsh-wiggle from Narnia,
Only my brother.
He's not a dirty pig from the pen, (actually, he is!)
Only my brother.

Paras Junejo (11)
Cardiff High School

THE SWEETS I LIKE

I love millions, small and sweet,
Chocolate mice are all I want to eat!
Nerds and Dweebs are sweet and sour,
I can eat loads within the hour!
Milky Buttons are really yummy,
I want them all in my tummy!
Flying saucers fly in space,
But I could murder a strawberry boot lace!
Cabbage makes me really sick,
But lollies are all I want to lick!
Sherbet gives me a fizz,
But cola bottles are the biz!

These are the sweets I really liked,
When I was a little tyke!

Joanna Borley (11)
Cardiff High School

SUMMER IS . . .

Summer is a burning blanket of fire,
A golden furnace,
Like a bubbling saucepan it boils,
Rainbows form
And spread happiness in its path,
Reds, yellows and oranges,
Burst into action,
Roses crack the earth and sway gently,
Slowly leaves begin to fall,
Death is born.

Jenny Newcombe (12)
Cardiff High School

Colours

Blue like the sea so sparkly and clear
White like an eye which might form a tear.
Colours all different from each other
Each day I want to see another.

Yellow like an egg yolk surrounded by white
I don't like eggs, but then again you might.
Orange like an orange all juicy and round
When you eat one it makes a funny squishing sound.

Black like the day when the sun burns out
That will be the day when we'll panic, scream and shout.
Green like leaves, which, on trees would grow to the top
I'm afraid this poem must now stop.

'This is a test?' someone mutters
Well, I think I've passed with flying colours!

Martin Potter (11)
Cardiff High School

A Picture Of A Horrible Monster

Its eyes are like eggs bulging out of its sockets.
Its teeth are like beetles crawling around.
Its tongue is like a snake:
Its body is like a ball of slime
And its feet too small to hold it up.
But it was just my sister.

Sam Price (11)
Cardiff High School

LUST

The sun sets,
The clouds dissolve.
The sea encompasses the land,
The sky is red,
The sea alight.
Folds of scarlet lap at the sand.
Like a bath of blood,
The waters gurgle with venom.
Effervescent and alive,
It crashes to the shores,
Exploding like gunpowder at the foot of the cliffs.

The rock bleeds itself dry.

Nadia Kidwai (16)
Cardiff High School

BLACK PILLAR

The fresh sea wind blows from afar.
The country manor house is waking up,
While destruction and havoc is caused,
By hurricane winds and pounding rain,
It is still standing proud throughout.
It is being tickled left, right and centre,
From raindrops racing to the ground.
Its arms are beginning to weaken,
Cracks appear by its shoulders.
Its strength evaporating, it falls to the ground,
Defeated by the wind.

Andrew Scott (16)
Cardiff High School

WAR

Crash,
The sound rings throughout the night,
Bang,
The gunfire creates a new light,
Furious,
Vicious,
Like a red flame flower.
The planes whine and whiz,
Displaying awesome power.
The flower melts,
Into small red shards.
Shrapnel falling,
Into houses and yards,
The sky drips with blood,
That's mirrored on the ground.
Cities razed to mud,
Death all around
And when the sirens stop,
The destruction is laid bare.
Who will remember
The terror of the night,
When darkness ends
And dawn brings natural light?
Who will remember
The terror of war and pain?
Please never forget,
What man in evil does.
Please never forget,
War.

Jayne Lutwyche (15)
Cardiff High School

UNCLE PHIL

When I was younger,
He would pretend his half a finger hurt him.
I would touch it gingerly
Then he would yelp, grinning at me.
He always plays jokes on me,
Shows me tricks to play on others.
He has many talents,
For example, he's an ace juggler
And a first rate musician.
In appearance, he's not too tall
And not too short.
Tall enough for me to hug him,
Without him having to bend over too far.
His bright, sharp eyes are keen, watchful.
I rarely see him though,
As he lives in London,
Although he was born in Ireland.
He hasn't lost his quiet, Irish accent,
Despite all the different accents he lives amongst.
Cockney, Welsh, Scottish, English,
He's him, an individual
And I like him like that.

Josie Britton (11)
Cardiff High School

YELLOW, SHINING LIGHT

Eyes are like yellow, shining lights,
Teeth are like daggers,
Ears are like pointy dwarf ears,
Hair is like a ragged cloth.

Legs are like stone.
Feet are stiff and muscly,
Head is like an egg,
Nose is like a round, squashed cherry.

Damian Griffiths (11)
Cardiff High School

LIFE CHOICES

Each move we make
Determines our next.
Each path we take
Determines our breaks.

Life is a loose track
Through a thick wood,
No set path for us to take
But so many choices for us to make.

Some will lead to a better life,
Others will take you into more strife.
But be sure of this, the choice you make
Will give you another with equal stakes.

Every second you wait,
Every choice you dismiss,
Another is created
Full of opportunity and heartbreak.

You can never be sure
Where each path will lead
But follow your heart
And I guarantee, you'll succeed.

David Lloyd (16)
Cardiff High School

UNCLE BERNARD

As I looked out of the train window,
I saw him running towards me.
His trainers white as snow
And his suede Chinos as clean as his bald head.
He held out his arms and hugged me.
I remember his award winning Koi
Swimming happily in his tank
And his thrill endurance at Disney World
And the mega choc nut sundae at his favourite
Italian.
It's funny how his taste of music matches mine
Apart from the 70s music he likes.

Ben Pruchnie (13)
Cardiff High School

MIASMA

Out of my mansion,
A paved, empty street
He walks in silence.

Cold, smooth glass
Presses on my face
Rising above me.

Intimidation at the doorway -
Even before he enters
Evil is spreading.

The black pillar wins.

Lucy Shields (16)
Cardiff High School

Mummy's Boy

Daddy told me Mummy's pregnant,
She used to live with us,
Now she lives in a big white palace
With servants in navy dresses and white coats.
They serve her everything in bed
And she's got a television and a radio
And a room which she doesn't have to share with Daddy.
She's got a little red button which she presses
And all her servants come running.
They give her a bracelet to put on the top of her arm
And they fluff her pillows and rearrange the sheets for her.
People who I don't know come to worship her,
They leave offerings of fruit and flowers.
I know they're worshipping her because they just stare and smile
And don't say a word, exactly like we do in church.
She doesn't have to say thank you because she's asleep all of the time.
I think it must be lovely to get everything for nothing
And not have to say thank you
And get a nice new baby as a parting gift from the doctor as well.
I decided to be pregnant all my life when I'm older,
But when I told Mummy she just laughed and said
It wasn't worth the grapes and anyway I was a boy so I couldn't.
I asked why it mattered and she smiled and said
'You'll understand when you're older.'
I hate it when they say that.

Luci Ashley (15)
Cardiff High School

A STONE FOR A HEART

Standing on a cold, windy pebble beach
Skimming stones across the water
I look above at the bleak grey sky
Listening to the waves crash around me.

I look into my hand and scan with my eyes
I'm looking at my skimming stone.
It's cold, grey and motionless exactly like this very day
In anger I throw the stone away.

How I wish she still had her red heart,
The one that always cared.
Warm and full of life
Loving anything her loving eyes saw fit.

Her love for me is no longer like a red, red rose
But more like that cold grey stone that rested in my hand.
Just like that stone I threw her love away
And just like that stone she will drift away from me.

For me she has a stone for a heart
And she wishes that we could part.

Cameron Smith (16)
Cardiff High School

CAT

Its fur is as soft as velvet,
Its eyes are as green as emerald stars,
Its whiskers are as flexible as a bow of a string,
Its moves are as swift as the wind,
Its miaows are like a baby crying in a cot.

Saira Chaudhry (11)
Cardiff High School

THE ACCIDENT

The prick of a needle in my arm,
The doctor smiles, oh he's calm,
A small drop of blood.

My wheeled bed rolled like a coaster,
Into a room of fancy dress men,
Their knives are sharpened,
My arm lies dead,
I sink into blackness.

I wake up saddened,
But my arm remains,
The surgeons saved it from the savage beast,
The car that now rusts in the dead mechanised heap.

The other man's luck just ran out,
His heart machine 'bleep' breathed its last
And the rest that died, it wasn't my fault,
Their deaths rest in the other man's soul,
But remain as a phantom of my nightmares,
The accident.

Alex Roderick (16)
Cardiff High School

AUTUMN

Autumn is a crackling fire spitting flames,
Autumn is a carpet of golden leaves,
Autumn is a dark cloud raining colours,
Autumn is a time of death.

Charlotte Gaughan (11)
Cardiff High School

THE CALM AND THE DAY

The night-time moon floats softly over the town,
Shining her pale yellow light like a beautiful gown,
Surveying the calm and keeping it cool,
Her icy craters like mysterious pools.
Moon's soft presence licks the night air,
To disturb the peace, you would not dare,
For the atmosphere puts you in a trance,
As the stars in the sky do their night dance.
All mystically twinkling, gently with wonder,
What sights and sounds do they encumber?

The wind quietly breathing through the trees,
Whilst it sleepily bounces around their leaves,
The houses stand dead,
The life is led
And the people are lifeless in bed.
Engrossed in their dreams,
All nonsense of course, but real they seem,
Like a rock though with a thought,
In a meaningless court,
Being shouted at by an imaginary judge,
Made up of pink fudge.
All nonsense, just like the sun,
Who destroys the calm for fun,
When it crashes in around six
With a flare and a kick
And exclaims life,
With a boiling white hot knife,

That the craziness we call day must start again
And so the people wake from their den,
Called slumber,
With such a blunder,
That the calm is utterly forgotten
And in its wake, the stress of day begins one more time,
How utterly rotten!

Jamie Sloan (13)
Cardiff High School

A STONE FOR A HEART

Restricted by envy,
Held back by self disgust,
Thumping,
Hard against the anxious, concrete chest,
Pulsing -
Dark, cold messages to every nerve.

Jagged edges slash through meaty flesh,
Engraving meaningless outcries into the soul,
Imprisoned -
It cries for release,
Hungry -
It needs to be fed.

Insanity rages,
Burning deep within,
Engulfed in pain.
We watch -
The last drops, slowly, intensely fall . . .
Fading with the dust.

Fatima Bibi (16)
Cardiff High School

A BLOODY ACCIDENT

A small drop of blood,
Fell from his hand,
Ruby red and warm,
He shouldn't -
Not near those alleys,
Especially in the dark,
I could see the pain and anguish
Creep through his face,
Only small was the boy,
Insignificant to those around,
But the shock was enough -
I could see when we arrived,
But as we exited the hospital -
The small drop of blood had gone.

Jenny Petschenyk (16)
Cardiff High School

OH NO!

Its eyes are like slugs
Its teeth are like a wall of bricks
Its nose is like a stick
Its head is like a box
Its arms are like long wriggling worms
Its legs are like waving tree branches
Its hair is like guitar strings
Its chest is like a huge steel drum
Its ears are like tiny marbles
Its fingers are like fire sticks
Oh no I'm hidden, but it's seen me.

Toby Dovey (11)
Cardiff High School

THE RUGBY FAN

I sit in my reserved seat waiting for the
game to start,
I look around the stadium with pride
in my heart,
The whistle blows and my adrenaline pumps
And somewhere in the crowd a drum thumps.

They're close to the try-line and I get up
from my seat,
I start to sweat in the blazing heat.
They put the ball down and the crowd roars,
My face brightens and my spirit soars.

Because I am a rugby fan - passionate and true,
I support my country and city too.
Rugby is my life it's everything I do,
I hope this was an influence on you.

Thomas Shouler (14)
Cardiff High School

GREEN

Green is the colour of new leaves
blowing in the summer breeze.
It is an apple hanging on a lime green
tree.
The grass is the emeralds gleaming
of the sun's reflection.
Green is of a bottle being recycled.
The pea is like a speck on the floor
ready to be squashed.

Joel Elmer (11)
Cardiff High School

FEAR

The gigantic shiver running down your spine,
That haunting scream, and high pitched whine.
The uncontrollable wretch at the back of the throat,
The car crash victim and overturned boat.
The creaking stairs and dripping tap,
The knocking at the window, the rap, rap, rap.
The ghostly shadows, short and stout,
The darkness falls, there's no way out.
You dare not move, never mind cough,
The phone lines are cut, and the lights are off.
You're all alone no one's near,
You tilt your head you can almost see her.
There's someone here, you know they're here,
You turn the corner and you're facing your fear!

Kate Gordon (15)
Cardiff High School

SPRING IS . . .

Spring is the season of new life,
Awakening animals from their deep sleep,
Telling everyone that winter is over,
Blossoming trees flutter in the gentle breeze,
Daffodils slowly open their yellow buds,
Whilst the baby lambs skip around the crowded fields.
How I love spring,
When the sun is warm
And winter is past memories.

Alicia Eccles (12)
Cardiff High School

A Day That Ends All

A cold day in the eyes of a child,
Even though the sun is beating down hard.
A lonely day in the eyes of a child,
Even when surrounded by people.
A cold and lonely day, but why?
Because the merciless bullets make it cold
And the dead bodies make it lonely
And the beautiful fresh green grass that was,
Is now suffocated with a sheet of bright red blood
And the glistening blue eyes of an innocent child
That were once so full of happiness,
Are now empty.
People who were at peace,
Now die.
The future is dark for the orphan
And hopeless for the people.
Maybe to die
Would resolve all differences.

Nadia Ameer (15)
Cardiff High School

Bully

Scared mind, green eyes
Punch, punch.
Red hopes, fallen dreams
Punch, punch.
Blue dreams, drowned heart
Punch, punch.
Yellow limbs, hiding behind a kick
Punch, punch.

Jessica Wilson (13)
Cardiff High School

THE SEA

An endless blue carpet
Melting into the clear sky
The sun stares vainly at its reflection
Whilst the wind crinkles its mirror.

A tiger is chasing me
It gallops along the shore,
Until its roaring mouth breaks into a foam
It growls as it softly slips away.

Sunset dawns
The sun's light gently fades
As it sinks into its deep bed
And darkly sleeps until morning appears.

Josie Satchell (15)
Cardiff High School

SPACE POEM

As I opened my eyes
I saw black and planets around the solar system
Stars twinkled and sparkled
A chill was in the air
The sun was like a great ball of fire
Running through the sky.
Suddenly a red planet erupted
And hot lava spat by me
Then it all stopped
I opened my eyes and the dream was over.

Louise Parry (12)
Cardiff High School

MY BOX

Into my box,
A cardboard brown box
With weathered corners
And sticky tape seals,
I place my memories
Of people who knocked it
As they rambled through my room,
Of conversations soaked up
By its Dairy Milk walls,
Of childhood holidays,
Where it housed our toys.
And so this box of nostalgia
I place in a quiet corner of my room,
Because my box isn't a performer,
It's an observer of life.

Sana Kidwai (15)
Cardiff High School

CLENCH WITH ANGER

Its eyes are like the glowing stars at night,
Its teeth are as sharp as daggers,
Its skin is covered in green slime,
Its booming voice echoes far and wide,
Its black nails are so long they curl over,
Its heavy feet shake everything when it walks,
Its wrinkled hands clench with anger
As it walks towards me.

Sophie Marshall (11)
Cardiff High School

IF I COULD COMPARE THEE

If I could compare thee to anything
What would I compare thee to?
A gentle summer breeze, which cools you but keeps you warm
A single red rose to show her beauty and perfection
A star who never stops sparkling even in the dark
But if not those then what?
As Shakespeare once said
'If music be the food of love, play on.'
For now I have lost the will to live
She is perfect in all ways and gives her best in everything
And how could I have ever deserved such a creation like her
Only she knows.
Now that she has left
I shall compare thee to the world
Because that's what she meant to me.

Ayotunde Adebanjo (17)
Cardiff High School

WHAT IS GREEN?

Green is,
the grass which dances in the summer air.
It is the emerald green on the apples
that dangle from their tree.
The pea pods being ready to burst
out into a frenzy of life
and the giant redwood's leaves
gulping up the billowing breeze.

Rhys Thomas (11)
Cardiff High School

SPACE POEM

In the dark, colossal nothingness of space,
The eternal peace is breathtaking,
Here civilisation means nothing
As earth has disappeared,
The sun, now just a pea,
Grows old and dims
To just a flicker of light
Like a glo-worm passing away,
When I stare up to the heavenly bulb above,
Growing larger and larger,
My hope is silenced,
As it is dark and dead,
Just like the last one!

Michael Rose (12)
Cardiff High School

CREATURES OF THE SEA

In the sea and far below
To another world where we can go,
To see the creatures of the deep,
Where fish can leap and hide and seek.
Little fish are staying together,
Safety in numbers against the predator.
The shark swallows them in great hunger,
A shame it was a great number.
I hope one day that there will be,
As many creatures of the sea,
For future generations to see.

Nadine Aburas (13)
Cardiff High School

A SMALL DROP OF BLOOD

A small drop of blood
Drops to the ground
The little boy gives out
A deafening sound

A small drop of blood
Fills the air
Innocent killed
But no one cares

A small drop of blood
On ward number three
No one feels the pain
Apart from me

A small drop of blood
Falls during the fight
Everyone turns away
From the sickening sight

A small drop of blood
Comes down from the crash
The old man's life
Is lost in a flash

A small drop of blood
Is lost in battle
The soldiers run
Like stampeding cattle

A small drop of blood
As the mother falls to her knees
There is something crying
Inside me

A small drop of blood
Trickles from the thorns
It is as if
They are the devil's horns

A small drop of blood
It doesn't hurt much
But if you're not careful
You'll feel the devil's touch.

Steven Hartshorne (13)
Cardiff High School

SPACE

As I looked up into space through my telescope,
I was amazed at what I could see,
I could see the darkness of space,
The stars were twinkling everywhere,
There were planets spread out all over,
Space was endless,
There was no sound,
No movement,
Then I spotted an unusual shaped object moving around,
Inch by inch,
It started moving faster,
It was getting closer and closer,
I looked away from my telescope,
I heard a loud squeaking noise,
I leaped to my telescope and there was nothing there.

Zubair Sheikh (13)
Cardiff High School

No More Skies

No more skies forever
No more skies again
No more skies forever
Never and the same
No one holds the winter
Winter is a game
Touch the icy beauty
Never be the same
Take my hand, you'll rest assured
You assert your evil plans
Touch the arms of winter
Held as you go down
Restless hands and tired minds
The beauty slows me down
Hold on to your evil dream
Winter is a frown
Hope for skies forever
Hide to hide and seek
Found you now that danger's close
The beauty falls asleep.
Poison drives the winter nights
Touched you to your soul
Push the gales and make a stand
The kingdom overthrown.

Christina Constantinou (14)
Cardiff High School

THE MILLENNIUM STADIUM

You walk in the gate,
Then up the stairs,
As you listen to the cheer of the fans.

With red tops on
And a smile on their faces,
The fans seeing Wales play.

Through the doors,
You meet a blinding light
And your eyes are filled with an incredible sight.

There before you lies a field of green
And a sea of red with faces,
Gazing upon the scene.

When you sit down,
The atmosphere embraces
And then the time has come for the match to start play.

As the ball is kicked,
Cheers arise,
The cheers for Wales, their homeland and pride.

As more tries are scored,
We know we can win,
Let's not throw this victory into the bin.

The whistle sounds,
That's it, we've won,
Let's come again for another one.

Jonathan Butters (14)
Cardiff High School

SPACE!

As I stand by the curtain, I look up so high,
So high in the dead, midnight sky,
I look past the aeroplane's invisible road,
And past where the graceful birds fly.

Has anyone ever told you about my great eyesight?
I can see Pluto, Jupiter and Mars,
All this from the room, where I stand
And in great detail, I can see the stars.

I can see the flaming red planets,
Coloured like a leaf, in an autumn tree,
Some planets are very cold,
Their colour, like the deepest blue sea.

You may think my eyesight is unusual,
But I'm angled in a slope,
That means I'm not human or animal,
Yes, of course, I'm a telescope!

Vicky Stollery (13)
Cardiff High School

SPACE POEM

Space is a lonely place,
A star to keep me company,
In this dark, vast and silent place,
There lies an alien.
It sleeps soundless in outer space,
It wakes, its tentacles tingle,
It stares at me,
Looks like that's it for me.

Karen Baker (12)
Cardiff High School

GRAVITY

What would happen if there was no gravity?
Cars would sail silently past,
causing no pollution.
In autumn, the leaves on the trees wouldn't fall,
they'd just float around forever,
and pupils would fly to school!

Mind you . . .

How would you park the car?
Eating spaghetti could get messy
and the bolognese would give you more than
just a saucy moustache
But, how on earth would you
go to the toilet?

Andrew Budd (13)
Cardiff High School

BLUE

Blue is
The shoes that patter in the rain
It is the sky that moves with the wind,
It is the ink that blots my work,
And the punk's hair that stands out in the street,
I watch the bluebells bursting with energy
And the sea, smooth as glass,
My soul is calm.

Vicky Wright (11)
Cardiff High School

HOW TO SPEAK ALIEN

If you want to speak alien,
This is what you do:
But mark my words,
Most of this poem is a load of
gobble di goo!

'Thank you' *is* 'Fomgobble whiz,'
'Please' is 'gomesh'.
If you want to say
'I'll have the roast duck'
Then just shout out 'Cobaflesh.'

'My name is . . .' translates to 'Zindoo'
'What is your name' is 'Hanygan'
If you want to say
'I'll buy that, please!'
Then just shout out 'Gomeshficwan.'

Eric Wilkins (12)
Cardiff High School

THE SEASIDE

We set off to sea on a summer's day,
It was boiling hot and in the middle of May.
I got on my bathers and went in the sea.
A shark ate my brother and then came for me.

After my swim I started to dig a hole,
Out of the sand popped a crab named Noel,
He nipped at my fingers and then at my toes,
I tried to get away but he got me on the nose.

It was dark now and time for the parade,
That theme was Posh Homes, there were butlers and maids.
I was really hungry now, I needed some grub,
We walked down the street and into a pub.

After our meal we got in the car,
On the way home I admired the stars.
It had been a truly wonderful day,
Even though my brother had sadly passed away.

Michael Godwin (13)
Cardiff High School

SPACE

'Where am I?'
I'm in a dark, empty, vast space
A quiet place
All I can see is black.
I turn around, I see Earth
I keep asking myself
Where am I?
Why have they sent me here?
What have I done?
What am I wearing?
I'm up in a suit
What kind of suit?
Am I going to die here?
Thinking all day long
Praying one day they will take me back to Earth
Until then all I will do is think and pray as hard as I can.

Sabrina Javaid (12)
Cardiff High School

WHERE IN THE GALAXY?

Tearing through the emptiness,
Where we go we couldn't care less,
Onwards, past the vastness,
To find eternal peace.

Power up and off we go,
Preparing for a terrific show,
Where we go, we don't know,
To find eternal peace.

It's like looking down a bottomless well,
Infinite, dark, has no smell,
The suns glisten like polished bells,
We'll find eternal peace.

Watching as the comets pass,
My life is going way too fast,
Don't look back, forget the past,
Over there, eternal peace!

I've found it now, (whoopee!)
Just eternal peace and me,
My life out here is totally free,
This is it, eternal peace.

Hector Wakefield (12)
Cardiff High School

REVENGE ON MY SISTER

Slug in a soup and succulent spider,
Bumblebee pizza and locust cider,
Dung beetle donuts and butterfly butties,
Stick insect sausage and ant avocado.

Joshua Parke (11)
Cardiff High School

SPACE

Space.
A huge black background with little white dots.
What are they?
Are they spaceships?
Are they alien planets?
Could they be burning gas balls or suns, each with other
galaxies of their own?
But when you see it explode,
Tons of pieces are flung into the outer reaches of space,
Or when you see a shooting star
The sight is a magical one.
Who knows what lurks behind the stars.
Aliens?
An exact replica of Earth?
I've always wanted to know but I doubt I'll ever.

Simon Bannister (12)
Cardiff High School

CATS

Eyes, like emerald headlights,
Fur, like velvet,
Legs, like springs,
Tail, like a liquorice whip,
Swishing like a windscreen wiper,
Moves like a tiger stalking prey,
Pounce,
The mouse is trapped.

Kate O'Grady (11)
Cardiff High School

SPACE POEM

A war has broken out,
And we have to leave home
To visit a world far from here
Where there is hope.

Looking out of the window,
I see space, dark and vast.
Nothing like my home,
Which is quickly now, only my past.

It's so quiet on the ship,
No one ever speaks.
Our hopes and futures gone,
All we have now is our dreams.

The shuttle lands;
I get butterflies in my stomach.
Our long journey is over,
All I have now is luck.

Rumana Malik (12)
Cardiff High School

YELLOW IS . . .

The glow of street lights as they switch into life at night.
A pride of golden lions lazing in the early evening sun.
A row of sunflowers wafting to and fro in the gentle breeze.
The sand between my toes as I walk along the beach.
When the moon starts to fall late at night.

Victoria Parker (11)
Cardiff High School

SPACE

The stars glisten like groups of holograms,
Earth rotates like a gigantic ball on a string,
Comets shoot by like fire bullets from a gun.
Space is too quiet,
too hot,
too dark.

I am all on my own, so sad and so tired,
I feel as though I have died
and taken the wrong turning,
I have no one to talk to,
no one to share my darkness with.
I hate space.
Space is too quiet,
too hot,
too dark.

Victoria Lane (12)
Cardiff High School

DINOSAURS

Herbivore or carnivore which will you be?
As long as a train or as tall as a tree.
You lived many years ago on Earth we know.
We've found fossils from head to toe.
Plates, spikes and tails you have on your back.
To stop some others to attack.
Some had teeth, others had claws.
You may have had none at all.
You were big, but your brain was small,
So now there's none of you at all.

Ashmere Sandhu (11)
Cardiff High School

INSIDE A BOX

If I could preserve the essence of the box,
The magical mystery of my memories,
Precious stories of my life to share,
Painful emotions of my past.
If I could only preserve a split second of these times,
to share the freshly-scarred wounds dug deep into my heart
with a sharpened blade.

Sweet melancholy called and drowned my soul,
And the bells tolled the second my nan passed away.
Silence bellowed in my heart,
And screams of anguish echoed in the hills.
Down I fell,
Down,
Down, as I curled up in a tatty, old, brown box.

Sarah Kiely
Cardiff High School

RED IS . . .

Red is . . .
Traffic lights on the massive Spaghetti Junction.
Blood from a man in battle.
Fruit falling ripe from the tree.
The fire bell ringing in a tall building.
The fiery glaze on the devil
It's the colour that children use most.
When I see it my heart beats faster!

Jason Porter (12)
Cardiff High School

School

Teachers shouting all the time,
Children chewing gum,
Homework handed in, in scraps,
Most not even done.

Litter dropped on the floor,
Graffiti on the walls,
Cramped, suffocating corridors,
Kids loitering in halls.

Children wearing trainers,
Shirts hanging out,
Teachers getting so annoyed,
They have to scream and shout.

Paper thrown around the room,
Teachers getting ignored,
Drawings on tables and chairs,
Children getting bored.

Bobak Batmanghlich (13)
Cardiff High School

Alsatian

Its fur is as soft as silk,
Its teeth are as sharp as fork lightning.
Its bark is a warning,
Its run is faster than light,
Its eyes are emerald green and they sparkle in the sun,
It's like my best friend I never had.

Charlotte Cameron (11)
Cardiff High School

I GOT THE BLAME

When my brother broke his arm,
When my homework came to harm,
And aliens visited my home,
And then landed on the Millennium Dome.
I got the blame!
Oh dear, what a shame.

When my guinea-pig ended up dead,
When she managed to dye my hair red,
And when the wedding cake went *splat!*
And landed on the bridegroom's hat.
I got the blame!
Oh dear, what a shame.

When a bomb exploded in my room,
When baby blew up due to food,
And the sun turned emerald green,
And I came home from space in a dream.
I got the blame!
Oh dear, what a shame.

Hannah Hanquing Zhu (12)
Cardiff High School

FEAR

So black.
It tastes of broccoli.
It is a scaled animal
Crying in the night
And feeling slimy.

Piers Smolinski (14)
Cardiff High School

SPACE!

We are aliens from outer space,
Sent here to destroy the human race,
Some are big,
Some are small,
Some are ugly and some are tall.

We are aliens from outer space,
We have lasers as big as the race.
The humans ran as quick as a mouse,
But we are quicker and wiped them out.

We are aliens from outer space,
Sent here to destroy the human race.
Now our mission is complete,
It's time to leave and finish in peace.

Poppy Muir (12)
Cardiff High School

THE MONSTER

Its eyes are like boils on the back of my neck,
Its teeth are rusty nails,
Its tongue is a slug,
Its tail, a spitting cobra
And its arms are slimy rat guts,
Its legs are spiky tree trunks.
It's a shame it's only an inch long!

Alec Magee (11)
Cardiff High School

LIFE

Life is like a turning key;
Unlocking new ideas and thoughts,
That are bursting to be told.

Life is like a rainbow;
All the majestic colours,
For all the different moods.

Life is a balloon;
If it is not held onto,
It leaves without a trace.

Life is like the sea;
Sometimes calm and pleasant,
But can be terrifying and dangerous.

Life is like a hurricane;
A twisting, turning nightmare,
That you'll never forget.

Mark Smith (14)
Cardiff High School

GREEN

Green is . . .
The sparkling emeralds that dangle from princess' ears,
While she lies on the luscious, soft grass in the springtime,
As the dark green leaves of the tree sway,
It drops a few juicy, green apples for the princess to eat,
As the world around her blooms in shades of jade and pink.

Sadia Kidwai (11)
Cardiff High School

SPACE POEM

Space the darkest, biggest place ever,
Space is the unknown,
With millions of stars and
One huge star,
The glowing star of the galaxy,
The burning balls of gas,
It's so bright it hurts to look,
It lights up the planets,
So everyone can see the millions of colours,
Red, blue, pink, purple and green,
It's all so beautiful.

Ryan Williams (12)
Cardiff High School

SWEETS GLORIOUS SWEETS!

Sweets glorious sweets,
Chocolate white mice which made me squeak,
Drumstick lollies I'd suck till they were bare,
Wildlife bars, I'd hope to get a tiger or cockatoo,
Rhubarb and custards after my danceclass,
Fizzy white and blue dolphins splashing
In the sea, wild and free!
Oh, sweets glorious sweets.

Kate Emma Griffith (11)
Cardiff High School

ALL ALONE

All alone on a sandy island
Moonlit pebbles beneath my feet
The roaring waves of the deep blue sea
in the distance
Clouds drawing in
Wind whispering in my ears
The sound of footsteps coming towards me.
Drawing nearer coming closer.
And *'Stop!'*
I hear no footsteps.
Was it my imagination?
Was it my ears playing tricks on me?
Somehow I don't think I'll ever know.
All alone on a sandy island.

Leanne Williams (12)
Cardiff High School

OBSERVATION

I place the scrunched up square teabag into the mug,
As I wait for the whistle of the kettle.
I pour the bubbling water and watch the clouds of steam rise.
The tea infuses into the scorching water,
Twisting like a whirlwind.
As I remove the soggy bag
The ice-cold milk hisses
As it hits the boiling water
And turns the liquid brown.

Kelly McIntyre (16)
Cardiff High School

SPRING

With rose petal slippers and a moss-covered gown
She mounts her silver stallion.
Breaking the curse of winter,
She rides the clouds in stately majesty,
Awaiting the call of her successor.

But who has seen spring?
For a cloth covers her face,
Which with its serene beauty
Can never be captured in any human eye.
For this is beauty that cannot be compared,
And with a wave of her wand,
A new life is formed.

Yet as soon as she has come,
She is gone,
And summer's hold
Leaves spring asleep for another year.

Rebecca Perry (15)
Cardiff High School

SYMPHONY IN BLUE

Topaz the stone of November,
Reminds me of cold winter nights,
The dark navy blue sky,
The stare reflecting in the aquamarine sea,
The sun wakens,
It brightens up the navy, starry sky,
To a bright sky blue
Where the stars shall hide.

Samantha Byrne (13)
Cardiff High School

TRAPPED

The dead of night,
Not a sound.
I'm all alone
In outer space.
This tunnel of darkness,
Longer and longer,
Forever as it expands.
I am lost,
Trapped in this tunnel of darkness,
Travelling to the unknown.

Louisa Guise (12)
Cardiff High School

MY BIG RED BOX

In my box I will put the taste of
tropical pineapple juice,
and the fresh relaxing experience of
Roath Park on a cold misty autumn morning,
and the smell of newly baked bread,
and the colour orange that holds
many brilliant feelings such as excitement!
I will close the box and let it drift in deep space,
forever preserving my thoughts and dreams.

Roger Barnfather (13)
Cardiff High School

WAR HEROES

Soldier stands,
Without his gun,
Heart in hands,
Till the job is done.

A feather for a medal,
He stands in line,
With all the brave others,
Who committed the crime.

Are the war heroes
The ones that fight the war?

Brave classed as weak,
Protecting the peace,
Upholding the justice,
Amidst the clouds so bleak.

Shot for their troubles,
They stood in line,
Refusing to fight,
In this dark, torn time.

Are the war heroes
The ones who fight the war?

James Kay (15)
Cardiff High School

THE BIG ONE

Nothingness,
Then with a huge explosion,
Bang!
Things flying everywhere,
The big bang,
Colourful atoms,
Stars being born,
Planets, forming and collecting,
Solar systems,
Galaxies,
Universes,
Wow!

Amazing,
Bright green and orange stars,
Whirling around,
Dragging planets towards them,
Planets
of all the colours in the prism,
Blue,
Lilac,
Red,
Green,
Purple,
Strange, mercy nebulae,
Floating in a black sea,
Small innocent asteroids,
Swimming like tadpoles in a vast lake,
Wow!

Grant Bassett (12)
Cardiff High School

AN ALIEN COMES TO EARTH

Great big towers on their side
Living in giant glass houses
Sleeping in very big houses
Going to and fro on big metal strips

In the glass house they eat
Tiny little things walk into them
Sometimes they don't like the food
So the little things walk out

When they wake up or finish eating
They don't thank anyone
Instead they shout and honk
And start going, slowly, then faster

For some strange reason
They can only go on strips
Sometimes there are three strips, not two
Nobody goes on three strip tracks

They themselves have lots of feet
And have little openings for the food
Usually they eat at the same time every day
But, sometimes they are late.

Simon Evans (12)
Cardiff High School

HATE

Hate is like a gun,
You never know when it will go off,
Taking out its hatred on the helpless.

Hate is like lightning,
Firing out at random,
You never know when it might strike.

Hate is like a spoilt child,
For once not getting his own way,
So he cries uncontrollably in a fit of rage.

Hate is like a thorn,
Suddenly it pricks you,
For no reason at all.

Hate is like a volcano,
Erupting on the wicked,
The judge and jury all in one.

Hate is a feeling,
Deep inside your body,
No one is safe where there is hatred around.

Settor Tengey (13)
Cardiff High School

DEPRESSION

Depression is a colourful canvas painted grey,
The taste of nothing where you expected everything.
It is the smell of all that you cannot have.
It looks like happiness locked behind a door.
It sounds like the same boring lecture over again.

Jon O'Neill (14)
Cardiff High School

IT WASN'T ME!

I didn't suffocate the dog,
Nor did I dissect the frog,
I didn't let the canary go free,
I'm telling you, it wasn't me!

I didn't hide a slug in his bed,
Nor did I step on the baby's head,
Of course I didn't drown the cat in the sea,
I'm telling you, it wasn't me!

I didn't swap worms for your spaghetti,
Nor did I say you looked like a yeti,
Of course I didn't shove his head in the potty,
I'm telling you! It wasn't me!

But,
All these things that I'm denying,
I think you've guessed that I am lying!

Alexandra Rose Meah (11)
Cardiff High School

SPACE POEM

All alone out here in space,
Empty, lonely and dark,
The only member of the human race,
Cries, whimpers and sobs,
He was sent out here for doing wrong,
Shouts and screams fill the vast space,
He'll never do the crime again.

Victoria Hunt (12)
Cardiff High School

SEASONS

Winter is a haggard old man
With a white snow beard
Blue icicle fingers
Dripping with frost
Sweeps over the world
Pulling his freezing blanket behind him.

Spring is a beautiful blonde
Dressed in a green dress of grass
Flower buds in her hair
Leading her flock of lambs
Through fields of new blossom.

Summer is a tanned brunette
Spreading her arms
Releasing sun rays
Tempestuous
She breathes her heat and colour
Onto the world.

Autumn is a curly redhead
Touching leaves to make them
Russet and brown
Knocking them from trees
As she twists and spins
Bringing the wind.

Hannah Wilcox (14)
Cardiff High School

ICE SKATING

My favourite hobby is ice skating,
I skate around happily.
With all the spins it makes me dizzy,
And all of the jumps and little twirls.

In competitions I sit and wait nervously,
Until my time has come,
I glide onto the ice and wait for my music to become,
And when it does I shimmer with fear,
With everyone watching me.
I ice skate past all the judges,
They are all looking at me.
I carry on until the music has stopped
Skating perfectly.

Once all the people competing have finished,
I wonder vigorously.
The judges read out the marks,
While the audience just sits silent and wait.
Yes, I've come first, I remark.
Skating back onto the ice,
I stand and get my medal,
With family taking pictures of me.

I have been to different rinks,
Bracknell, Basingstoke and many more.
I now skate for Cardiff but later I'm going to be skating for world.
I hope I win,
I like it so much,
The early morning lessons and the very little skirts.
With fun and joy with all my friends,
A target for the years.

Kimberley Johnson (13)
Cardiff High School

WAR

Death, hunger,
War, peace.
The fighting and sorrow will never cease.
Guns on the street lying around,
Dead bodies waiting to be found.
People of the town crying with pain
Losing their loved ones it will never be the same.
Arms and heads scattered over the floor,
Some from the rich and others from the poor.
Suddenly from behind, you hear a crack,
You know an innocent child is under attack.
Crunch all around you as the soldiers step on leaves,
A gentle echo as your child breathes.
A woman in front sobs and cries,
As all the people in the country die.

Ceri Jones   (13)
Cardiff High School

THE CAT

The cat's fur is as smooth
as the winter's snow,
It jumps like an angry lion,
its eyes are like the hazel bushes
in a beautiful garden,
The skin is as dark as the pitch-black night,
Anger is like the fiery breath of a dragon,
Teeth as sharp as a silver sword.

Ridah Bashir (11)
Cardiff High School

I Never Said That

I called him a dog
I called him a frog
I called him a rat
But I never said that.

I called her a snitch
I called her a witch
I called her a bat
But I never said that.

I called him betrayer
I called him a slayer
I called him fat
But I never said that.

I called her a liar
I called her false fire
I called her a cat
But I never said that.

John Pritchard   (14)
Cardiff High School

Green Is . . .

A bunch of grapes freshly picked from the vineyard,
It is the dew-covered grass waving in the wind,
I watch the trees as the jade leaves blow away,
It is the ripe green apple gleaming up at me,
My mum's emerald green eyes shining in the light,
I love green.

Rebecca Summerfield (12)
Cardiff High School

BLUE MEMORIES

Symphony blue,
It has many colours,
As I go back a long time ago,
I remember when I was young,
The blue breeze swaying the trees,
On a scorching day, summer's day,
Then I remember the blue of my quilt,
As I lie close to my comfortable bright blue quilt,
Then in the mornings when the sun is dawning,
As I decide what I have to wear,
I take out a warm navy blue jumper.
Then on the way to school
As I rush past the lake I see the royal blue lay effect,
On a cold winter's day.
I go back then to my first summer holiday
To when the sea was a clear turquoise as clear as can be.

Rosalind Smith (13)
Cardiff High School

BLUE IS . . .

A blot of ink on a white page
The baby blue skin of a smooth dolphin
A bluebottle gleaming in the morning rays
The sky a forget-me-not blue
Turquoise water glides over a sandy beach
Bluebells sway in the evening breeze
Powder blue calms my soul.

Taryn Kalami (11)
Cardiff High School

THE SEA

The sea
The deep blue sea
With a glimpse of silver
Twinkling with the sun which shines upon it.

The sea
The deep blue sea
Seems like an everlasting creature
Which never dies away or ever gets tired.

The sea
The deep blue sea
Full of all sorts of things
Like fish, octopuses, sharks and whales.

The sea
The deep blue sea
Full of mystery
And secrets of the Earth.

The sea
The deep blue sea
What lies beneath it?
It's all a secret, the sea is mysterious,
Swishing from side to side, rushing and pushing.
Brushing against the pebbles and shells
Washing them away.

The sea
The mysterious sea.

Saddiah Javaid (13)
Cardiff High School

MY CAT

The lazy old lump
Sits around all day
She doesn't move her rump
She never wants to play.

When she eats her food
She watches her back
Like she's in a mood
And we're going to attack

She stalks around
With her head in the air
And an arrogant grace all over her face
But look at her wrong
And she'll leave the ground
And sail through your legs in one giant bound

Our cat's a bit dull
She won't use the flap
We have to prop it open
She thinks it's a trap
She's absolutely terrified
Of every other cat
But we think she's the best
Despite all that.

Daniel Williams (13)
Cardiff High School

MY FAVOURITE SWEETS

The sweets I liked were

Flying saucers which flew in but never came out,
My multi-coloured ice lolly standing his stick,
Sherbet dib-dabs always made me cough.

Bought a packet of buttons just enough to share,
Push Pops, not so popular with my dentist
A Milky Way promised never to ruin my appetite!

Chewy eggs taste nicer than they sound,
Eat too many shrimps and I'd feel dizzy,
Chocolate pink pigs only on special occasions!

Where would I be without my sweets?

Kayleigh Walker (12)
Cardiff High School

THE THING

T hings live in your bedroom
H ide in your bed
E ach and every one eats lost toys!

T hey hate little children
H eads are square
I   n their mouths they have blue tongues
N o one's seen a thing (how do we know so much?)
G et things spray and frighten those monsters away.

David Burns (11)
Cardiff High School

MY LIFE

Born in Paris on a sunny day
While the children came out to play
Went back to Wales
To live in the valleys under the gales
Grew up in Rhiwbina
With my brother Andrew and sister Ana.

At the age of three
Enjoyed my Acorn Nursery
From toddler tears and snot
I finally left my cot
To jump on my surfboard
I glided over my primary years
Of work boredom and crisps
Splash with my friends in Llanishen pool
Kissed goodbye to my junior school
And now twelve going on thirteen
Cannot wait for my teens.

Daniel Munro (12)
Cardiff High School

THE SWEETS I LIKED WERE . . .

Milky Way bars, so that I could be blasted off into space,
Chocolate buttons, for when the real ones fell off.
Push Pops very sticky but fruity.
Dip Dabs because they fizzed up my nose,
The big cola bottles to keep me quiet,
Jelly Babies that wobbled inside me,
The really big gobstoppers, big enough to hide me!

Lucy Rogers (11)
Cardiff High School

SPIDER'S WEB

It glitters brightly in the morning,
When the dew has first come,
It sparkles like diamonds in a jeweller's stall,
It's silver and shiny and delicate too,
Like snowflakes falling from the sky,
It's like a five pence piece gleaming in someone's pocket,
It's like a maze with nowhere to go,
It's a beautiful, glittering, gleaming sparkling spider's web,
                                        that's what!

Stacy Halbert (11)
Cardiff High School

I WANNA BE RICH

I wanna be rich, don't wanna be poor
If I had a disease I'd then buy the cure.
I would buy clothes and be a cool dude
Mountains of drink and plenty of food.
I would have a big garden and a fine house
I would have a pet cow, a cat and a mouse.

Although I never go far
I would have a flash car.

Lewis Jones (14)
Cardiff High School

FEAR

Pale blue,
It tastes like weak tea that is cold
And smells like a musty room.
It looks frightened but frightening
And sounds like a starved cat.
It feels like a small animal trapped.

David Hughes (14)
Cardiff High School

WATERSKIING

I get in my life jacket and on my skies I jump
I leap in the water and I hear the engine bump
I grab the rope and off I go
Zooming along and a big wave shows
I go up like a rocket and to the left I glide
Off to the right and boy do I slide
Waterskiing is a lot of fun
When the sea is calm and there is plenty of sun.

David Roberts (11)
Cardiff High School

LIKE A WILTING ROSE

Like a wilting red rose
And tasting like a rotting dead corpse
And looks like starved children crying.
It sounds like the wails of suffering children.

Depression depresses me!

Matthew Barley (14)
Cardiff High School

RED ANGER

The taste of boiling hot soup.
The smell of a tramp.
An ugly, nasty monster
Looking like a spirit
Which inhabits my body.
The howling of a wolf
Under a full, winter's moon
While the fire is burning.

Kalpesh Kerrai (14)
Cardiff High School

THE JOURNEY

The day of the journey had finally come,
I said goodbye to my dad and my mum.
My mum smiled at me with a tear in her eye,
I gave her a cuddle,
She let out a sigh.
I told my mum I would be back soon,
I was only going to fly to the moon.

I got in the rocket,
And strapped myself tight.
I hoped it would be a comfortable flight.
I looked at my partner with a smile on my face.
I couldn't believe I was actually in space.
The journey would be over very soon,
After we had landed upon the moon.
I closed my eyes and then my mum said,
'Come on you lazy, get out of bed!'

Leona Richards (13)
Glan Ely High School

RUGBY WORLD CUP

The Millennium Stadium's finally done,
With a roof that opens to see the sun,
Graham Henry leads the way,
The whistle blows to start the play.

Robert Howley scores a try,
Neil converts it flying high,
In the game they play with pride,
With the ball right by their side.

Graham's smiling walking in,
Wales have won their tenth win.
The Welsh team are on the up,
Wales to win the Rugby World Cup.

Rebecca Green (12)
Glan Ely High School

ODE TO YOU

I'm alone . . . in a room.
I'm dreaming of you.
Your eyes like the midnight sky,
I'm thinking of you 'til it hurts.
Not even your kiss could ever delude me
You've got a life and it doesn't include me.
A tear runs dry on my face,
As I long for the warmth of your embrace.
I know in my heart that I'll never win you back,
She's got you now and that's why . . .
I'm alone . . . in a room.

Veronica Browning-Badey (13)
Glan Ely High School

HOMELESS

So sleepy,
So tired,
How I would love a bed,
Soft and comfy,
My own private space.
In need,
In hope,
Someone might save me,
From the loneliness of homelessness.
I look for scraps around in bins,
The shame.
So cold,
So wet,
The winter nights.
I'm hoping,
I'm dreaming,
Someone will save me,
Say I care,
I wish.
Please help me.

Carol Gronow (13)
Glan Ely High School

HAPPINESS

Happiness is the scent of wild flowers in a field.
Happiness is the swishing sound of the ocean waves.
Happiness is the taste of fresh summer fruits.
Happiness is the bright, glowing sunlight.
Happiness feels like warmth, wrapped around my skin.
Happiness is the world I like to be in.

Sheree Richards (12)
Glan Ely High School

The Snowman

Through the dried, tall weeds surrounded by sugar-coated trees
Crunching in the milky white snow
Unknown woodland creatures scampered from nearby shrubs.

A momentary pause to examine the shadow
Behind the iced bushes
Just imagination as a squirrel leaps
From one branch, breaking another.

Then a secluded plain with an emerging snowman
Melting in the ruthless heat that had boosted sky high.

Now my frozen friend is the size of a rabbit
Just managing to poke its head out of its grave
Looking like a postcard scenery glistening in the light.

The misty plump snowman now disappeared
From our icy world, back into his.

Diane Allen (13)
Glan Ely High School

Happiness

Happiness is smelling a hot roast dinner covered
                    with gravy on Christmas Day.
Happiness is snow falling, flake by flake
On top of treetops and on my warm hands.
Happiness is Wales scoring the winning try in the last few seconds.
Happiness is birds singing on a warm summer's day.
Happiness is cold pink ice-cream on a warm day at the beach.
Happiness is the greatest mood of all.

Stephen Ledley (12)
Glan Ely High School

ANGER

Anger is people lying dead
in the dryness of Sudan.

Anger is the blood and flesh
of a dead man.

Anger is war when people are
slaughtered to death.

Anger is touching the wounds
of people with hardly a breath.

Anger is the taste of bloody
salted meat.

Anger is beneath our feet.

Samantha Menzies (12)
Glan Ely High School

ANGER

Anger is the colour black, dull and dark,
Hiding everything inside.
Anger is a lion roaring and
Grinding his teeth in my ears.
Anger is a burning fire,
Burning up inside you.
Anger is a smell of smoke.
Anger has the taste of ash.

Anger means revenge.

Laura Taylor (12)
Glan Ely High School

HAPPINESS

Happiness is the bright sun shining on me.
Happiness is the waves crashing on the sand.
Happiness is fresh roses.
Happiness is ice-cream on a hot sunny day.
Happiness is silk all over my soft skin.
Happiness is the mood I'm always in.

Nicola Jones (12)
Glan Ely High School

FEAR

Fear of hyenas eating a zebra,
Fear of haunting ghosts,
Fear of a deadly fever,
Fear of burning toast,
Fear of someone watching you.

Fear is always there, somewhere!

Kelsie Dyer (12)
Glan Ely High School

ANGER

Anger is God throwing sharp forked lightning across the sky.
Anger is a small secret locked up inside.
Anger is a small child crying for its mother.
Anger is a bitter lemon on a slice of bread and butter.
Anger is the smell of a blood red flower, dying in the summer sun.
Anger is a mood caused by my brother.

Emma Beech (12)
Glan Ely High School

FEAR

Fear is a big bloodied, bruised body
buried in a coffin.

Fear is the smell of fresh blood
dripping from a person.

Fear is the burning blaze
in the pits of hell.

Fear is the taste of poison ivy
sizzling in my mouth.

Fear is a helpless animal being caught
in a poacher's trap.

Fear is my mum.

Matthew Stevens (12)
Glan Ely High School

HAPPINESS

Happiness is me eating my garlic pizza
Happiness is me torture racking my sister
Happiness is seeing my sister walking
Happiness is hearing my sister talking
Happiness is the smell of cakes cooking
I'll be lucky to get a look in.

Ross Penfold (12)
Glan Ely High School

THE MILLENNIUM

The millennium is nigh,
Everyone will be cheering so will I.
Henry VIII went through women fast,
And men wore ruffs but that soon became the past.
The black death killed one person in three,
And pirates fought all over the sea,
And we mustn't forget the legendary Robin Hood,
And the magna for King John to promise to rule good.
William Shakespeare wrote many famous plays,
And the gunpowder plot failed in so many ways.
Florence Nightingale nursed soldiers in the Crimean war,
And Emmeline Pankhurst fought for women's rights
And that soon became the law.
We mustn't forget Titanic which perished with gloom,
And Neil Armstrong who was the first man on the moon.
With the Dome almost on its feet,
I would say the millennium is almost complete.

Danielle Cross (12)
Glan Ely High School

ANGER

Anger is the deadly colour red.
Anger is dogs that have never been fed.
Anger is like rotting meat.
Anger is like stinking hot feet.
Anger is like someone screaming,
Anger is more than a feeling.

Katie Wright (12)
Glan Ely High School

HAPPINESS

Happiness is the sight of a smile on a baby's face.
Happiness is the sound of friends having fun.
Happiness is a smell of roses glowing in the dark.
Happiness feels like the warmth of cotton wrapped around my skin.
Happiness is like the taste of fresh tea and breakfast in the morning.
Happiness is the mood I love to be in.

Hayley Purse (13)
Glan Ely High School

HAPPINESS

Happiness is the sound of my brother laughing
Happiness is the taste of ice-cream on a hot day
Happiness is the touch of my nan's hands when I am lonely.
Happiness is the sight of my mum when I'm homesick.
Happiness is the smell of my dad's curry when I am hungry.

Happiness is what my mum likes to see me as.

Nicola Osman (12)
Glan Ely High School

THE OCEAN

In the ocean lies an ocean bed where whales live their peaceful slumber.
Dolphins dance in schools of joy.
Sharks are biting, giving birth, eyes awaken to Mother Earth.
Sea snakes lurking in the gloom, little fish await their doom.

Tyrone Herbert (11)
Whitchurch High School

School's 'In' Again!

Off goes the alarm clock,
Buzzing in my ear,
Lovely day outside,
Pity! I'm not going to enjoy it,
School's in again!

Sun shining off the windows,
Gleaming off the pond,
Red leaves litter the path,
The swans sing their song,
Pity! I'm not going to enjoy it,
School's in again!

1st lesson not bad,
2nd hell,
3rd lesson torture,
4th lesson where's the bell!
5th lesson terrible,
Will it never end?

Finally it's over,
Running home for tea,
Happily a bird sings flying past me,
But tomorrow has to come,
Another day to face,
But looking at my diary,
See the smile on my face,
It's Saturday tomorrow,
Ice skating I'll have to face!

Louise Spinola (13)
Whitchurch High School

SCHOOL

A way to get us out of the house,
A way to make us pay,
A way to trap us like a mouse
From day to day to day.

Time to teach the world we're ready,
Time to make them pay,
Time for the plan, on your marks, steady.

They say it's for our future,
They say it's for our sake,
They say to listen to the tutor
And not to make a mistake.

Tyrone Gharibi (13)
Whitchurch High School

THE COUNTRY

The tall trees where birds sing out loud,
As sheep in the field say, 'Baa.'
The grass waves back and forth as the sun sets,
Moorhens drinking from the slow flowing river,
As puddles are broken apart by children playing.
The cows go to sleep,
As the bright, glowing sun gives its last shine.
The farrier calls his children to come in.
It goes dark and starts to rain.

Patrick Howell (13)
Whitchurch High School

ALONE

The stadium is in the city centre,
Alone and talking to the air,
The skyscraper standing proud,
Piercing the mist above,
He can only look at the foliage and their friends,
Alone watching,
The motorway is busy and not alone,
Until the night he is alone,
He can only look at the river beneath and dream
         he could move.
The puddle is lonely and waits for rain,
The candle is alone and very sad and soon he
         will be no more.

Robert Critchley (13)
Whitchurch High School

CITY RAIN

Clouds come from above
like a black bull raging in the sky.
But then suddenly water drops from
the sky for weeks on end.
The rain suddenly stops and
the savage bulls move away.
The sun comes out and brightens up the sky.
The city brightens up as the sun dries away
the rain, as the city comes alive once again.

Christopher Smith (12)
Whitchurch High School

TYPHOON

People playing on the beach, having fun, a dollop each
Building castles in the sun, ice-cream, lollies, yum, yum, yum.

The sun goes in and it's no longer dry, the sea rises to an all time high.
Down comes the rain, hard and wet, soaking the people, they're
angry, I bet.

Out on the horizon, growing big, tall and strong, is a mountainous
wave as tall as Snowdon.
A surfer strolls up, to conquer his fear of drowning in waves so high
and so sheer.

Typhoon by nickname, but calm now within, the surfer surveys the
scene before him.
His eyes watch for breaks in the pounding white foam, his heart's
pumping wildly - why wasn't he home?

The right wave comes nearer, and typhoon gets set, his board waxed
so well it seems not to get wet.
He paddles and moves to the perfect position, this one is just right -
an instinctive decision.

The wave's here, it's reached him, it's ever so strong, he stands tall
and proud as it speeds him along.
He's done it, he's surfed it, and he's beaten his fear. His mates, who
are watching, let out a cheer.

No more will he worry when bullies play 'slaughter', on account of
his crazy, mad fear of wild water.
His surfing exploits mean they go away soon, and he really lives up
to his nickname, Typhoon.

Luke Nash (12)
Whitchurch High School

BONFIRE NIGHT PARADE

Bang!
A spectacular show has started,
Bright sparks form wheels in the night,
Red, yellow, green and blue,
Light up the dark, ebony sky.

Bang!
There goes another one,
This time it's gorgeous violet.
As the light parade begins,
A fiery furnace starts to flame.

Bang!
A little yellow light
Goes shooting to the sky.
As the silver sparkles tumble,
Amazement strikes from wall to wall.

As the party comes to a close,
Exciting thoughts tingle the toes.

Christine James (12)
Whitchurch High School

SILAGE IN THE COUNTRYSIDE

While the ground lays flat,
The cows give it a pat.
I shout 'Daisy! How dare you?'
But she just gives me a 'moo'.

The smell is disgusting,
Quick run away,
It's running towards us,
Nothing can stop it.

As the whiff drifts across the fields
Like an aeroplane in its flight,
It smells like an animal corpse,
It's that bad.

As the smell goes away,
It very slowly fades,
I hate it when that happens,
I really, really do!

Rhys Heal (13)
Whitchurch High School

THE DESERT

The desert, a barren land,
Where only a few plants grow.
A place where I am on my own.
The sun shining down,
The tremendous heat.
I pray for rain.
Nothing to drink , just a dirty trough.
No food will grow.
I pray for rain.
My prayers have been answered,
the rain has come.
I rejoice.
Some food has grown,
We drink.
I save some for another day
when it is hot.
The animals drink.
I am happy.

Estelle Stock (12)
Whitchurch High School

RAIN

The rain beats down on the corrugated roof,
It trickles down the drainpipe,
And into an old bucket.
The bucket overflows,
And sneaks down the drain.

The rain rushes in, like an express train
On its way to a collision.
The rain comes down with even more speed,
Then the sun shines through
And the rain sneaks down the drain.

The rain slows down . . . for a while,
Then comes down heavier still.
The rain comes to an end.
The sun appears from behind a cloud
And the rain . . . is gone!

Tim Mordecai (13)
Whitchurch High School

THE VOLCANO!

A mist has come over the land,
A smell of destruction is here,
At sunset we shall all be waiting,
For the end of our peaceful town.

It brings mass destruction to the land,
And burns everything in its path,
Yes it is a *volcano!*

Rhys Oxenham (12)
Whitchurch High School

MY BIRD (SO HIGH)!

Oh bird you fly so high,
You fly so high, so high in the sky.
Gliding so fast,
You wish it would last.
Dodging the clouds,
You look so proud.
Flapping your wings,
I love it when you sing.
Tweeting a song,
You'll never go wrong.
Looking so sharp for something to eat,
It is so easy when you have a sharp beak.
Oh my bird flying so high,
Flying so high, so high in the sky.

Jamie-Leigh Deane (12)
Whitchurch High School

WATER

Water, what is water?
Rain, snow, typhoons and hurricanes, they all contain water.
The drink you drank last night, the drink you drank this morning.
The food you ate last night, the food you ate this morning.
The rain which splashes on your head, the rain that splashes on
the floor.
You cannot live without water, it's everywhere.
It's in your body,
It's in your mouth,
It's down the drain,
It's in your brain. Water it's everywhere!

Rhydian Parry-Owens (12)
Whitchurch High School

BONFIRE NIGHT

November 5th, Bonfire Night,
Catherine wheels turning,
Bonfires burning,
Fireworks crack and light up the sky,
Sparklers alight, as bright as the sun.

Firework displays are put on for the children,
Fireman aside to put out the flames.

Red, purple, green and blue,
Orange, yellow, pink and brown
Are the colours we see.

Guy Fawkes is fun,
But safety comes first.

As the night goes by
The wind gets rough.
At the end of the night water is used to
                              put out the flames.

Donna-Marie Huntley (12)
Whitchurch High School

MY BEDROOM

Inside my bedroom lies a planet which is far away from Earth.
On my bedroom floor lies the messy side of me,
Below my bedroom lies a deep, dark land,
Above my bedroom a paradise of happiness,
Next to my bedroom is a mad and weird place,
Past my bedroom is a place where I can get away from the world.

Nadia Refae (11)
Whitchurch High School

THE SEASONS

January, February sometimes March,
A cold, frozen person walks about the place,
Freezing things, killing all the plants,
Stripping the trees bare,
Putting most of the animals to bed,
You ask, 'Who is this mean person?'
I answer, 'It's not a person, it's winter.'

March, April and May,
A warm, wet person hops about the place,
Warming things up, bringing life to plants,
Putting leaves and blossoms back on the trees,
Waking animals up and bringing new life to mothers,
You ask, 'Who is this jolly person?'
I answer, 'It's not a person, it's spring.'

June, July and August,
A hot person who runs and laughs about the place,
Making things hot, making all the flowers grow,
Putting fruit on the trees,
All the animals are out playing.
You ask, 'Who is this hot person?'
I answer, 'It's not a person, it's summer.'

September, October, sometimes November,
A warm, cold person walks about the place,
Cooling things down,
Killing the plants, turning all the leaves into a rainbow,
Then stripping them.
You ask, 'Who is this person?'
I answer, 'It's not a person, it's autumn.'

Then we go back to winter. These are all the seasons in
                                    the order they come.

Fiona Edwards (14)
Whitchurch High School

FIRE

The sun is a big, ball on fire,
It's scolding hot,
It's a bright fluorescent orange,
November 5th comes,
Bonfire Night,
Everybody crowds around
while it burns the
rubble away.
Sparks on the fire fly off the
Catherine wheel.
Children look in amazement.
People burn candles
to relax them
or even to release
a smell into the atmosphere.
A house on fire
is dangerous,
It can kill you.
Never put anything but
water on the fire.
Never play with matches.
Fire is scolding hot,
Fire is a bright, fluorescent orange.

Catherine West (12)
Whitchurch High School

TIGERS

Orange as the sun,
It jumps in and out of trees,
like wind it runs
after the helpless prey,
its teeth sharp as swords.

Its black and orange body
wanders in the jungle.
Its belly full of prey,
it slowly goes to sleep.

Sarah Stinton (11)
Whitchurch High School

SEASONS' SUBTLETIES

For winter, it is a deadly sin,
With its bitter cold wind, it does bring,
Travelling the world in its chariot throne,
All the way from the arctic zone.

For spring has a wonderful feeling,
Underneath the ground, the moles are tapping the earthy ceiling,
Baby lambs and a brand new flower,
Blinded by the sun, away they cower.

For summer is a lovely thing,
With birds singing the songs they sing,
Barbecues and lazing in the blazing sun,
Bringing joy to everyone.

For autumn is so lovely,
It leaves you feeling bubbly,
Bonfires and falling leaves,
Catch one and make a wish is believed.

For winter it is a deadly sin,
With its bitter cold wind, it does bring,
Travelling the world in its chariot throne,
All the way from the arctic zone.

Rebecca McCrann (13)
Whitchurch High School

AUTUMN

Autumn has come, trees looking bare,
Leaves covering the ground like different coloured hair,
Animals are ready for their winter sleep,
Coldness comes which makes poor children weep,
The Earth starts to give us bad weather like storms,
While people have fires to keep them warm.
Flowers are dying, clouds are black,
Children are wearing kaleidoscope hats.
Autumn is the season for Hallowe'en,
When ghosts and goblins are often seen,
Autumn leaves are like a crumpled up sheet,
Where people come and crush them with their feet.

Lucy Bird (13)
Whitchurch High School

THE MOUNTAIN

Standing tall and steep,
With their high, sharp tops
And snow covered ground.
Watching over the rocky hillside
With its steep, slippery slopes
And its grey and brown rocks.
Watching over the gentle hillside
With its lush green meadows
And its rivers and valleys.
Looking up at snow covered mountains.

Tobias Holmes (13)
Whitchurch High School

Autumn Evenings

Autumn comes and trudges on,
A dull, old man his youth now gone.
His cloak of leaves lay like a rug,
This last blaze of fire awaits the flood.
Silver grey hair flutters in the sky,
A smoky, black beard floats from chimneys high.
Then stumbling through the icy air,
He dulls our warm hearts without a care.

We seek the glowing refuge of home,
I sit by the fire with scarlet cheeks,
And remember the joys of the summer weeks.
From the cocoa I take a sip,
Outside the windows begin to drip.
Autumn comes and trudges by,
A dull, old man who waits to die:
And when he's gone and snow is here,
He finally sleeps for another year.

Joe Tandy (13)
Whitchurch High School

The World

Far from the world lies emptiness and nothing,
Close to the world is a breathable atmosphere.
Above the world are clouds, sun rays and thunderstorms.
On the world are blue oceans and waves.
All around the world, people unfortunately pollute her,
But, somewhere on the world, somebody is helping her stay alive.

Dafydd Salaman (11)
Whitchurch High School

AUTUMN'S END

Autumn is a season unlike any other,
The tree leaves once green, are now red and orange,
The colours of fire.
The branches spreading out above you, like a thousand hands,
All trying to touch one another,
But not succeeding.
The ground beneath your feet, wet with dew,
Leaves crunch under foot as you walk along.
The wind moans as if it were weeping.
The vibrant summer colours of the flowers slowly disappears.
The hedgehog prepares his home for the coming winter months.
Birds fly away to seek better weather.
Winter draws near.
The artist's easel colours fade away,
Leaving nothing but dim shades of grey, winter is finally here.

Holly Slater (13)
Whitchurch High School

SPRING

As the ground's rid of its blanket of icing,
Spring is here, fresh and raining.
She walks through the lush grass,
As it swishes round her feet.
While the lambs are being born,
Cries of soft, gentle bleats.
The March wind blows through her soft, gentle hair,
The April showers, falling everywhere.
And as the March wind blows,
And the April showers,
Where would we be, without the May flowers?

Emily Graff (13)
Whitchurch High School

AUTUMN

Autumn arrives: she comes on the wind,
She announces her presence,
She whistles and sings.
Sweeping and swirling through fire-red trees,
She tears off the golden, fire-red leaves.
Down she swoops like a bird to its prey,
Scattering the leaves all different ways.
She leaves the world like a red and gold sheet,
Which rustles and crunches beneath people's feet.
When she returns, darkness she brings,
Casting a blanket of cold over all things.
As she spreads her sheets around,
Her friend crept up and put frost on the ground.
Together they make the world colourful and cold,
The memories of summer,
Now distant and old.

Samantha Arnold (13)
Whitchurch High School

THE OCEAN

In the ocean is a world of mystery
Below the surface small fish hide from predators
Above the ocean birds swoop and soar
On the ocean ships sail back and forth
At the shore, the ocean meets the land
On the shore, the ocean makes the sand
The ocean carries on for miles and miles
The ocean is a deep, dark place which supports life.

Christopher Powell (11)
Whitchurch High School

SUMMER HOLIDAY

Summer came again: happiness was there but heat was his tool,
It was that time of year again when he was made a fool.
He was spoilt 'surprisingly' with food, presents and a super jumbo gun,
But the joy of the atmosphere didn't spoil the fun.
People playing in the swimming pool and having barbecues when
                                                        it's cool.
There's nothing really better than a good holiday,
You can stay in or go out and play.
He is like the bright, shining sun,
Giving harmful effects out on everyone.
Bang, bang, bang went the big barrel gun,
The amazing thing was, that he could hold the ton.
It was a normal thing that he would annoy,
The neighbours around him with his new toy.
For people nearby it was still worth the wait,
That they could enjoy the six week break.
The red and yellows of the different coloured flowers,
Stand up straight like tall, huge towers.
Everyday people's spirits are still very high,
Until the time when sunset is nigh.

Joseph Dodd (13)
Whitchurch High School

THE DEEP BLUE SEA

Beneath the sea are the coloured pebbles,
which are beautiful and really smooth.

Above the sea are the loud seagulls,
which are scattering for food.

Below the sun are the rough waves,
which are crashing together.

In the sea are fish you've never seen before,
fat, thin, coloured, see-through, electrical.

Carly Jones (11)
Whitchurch High School

SPRING

Spring comes and the burning yellow sun comes out,
A sunrise over the valleys,
Shimmering through the trees
onto the lush green grass.
Water droplets run down the wet leaves
from the condensation that has occurred.
The sparkling frost in the early mornings
makes the world look like crystal ice.
A group of robins come out
and they are shadowing each other, around about,
so carefree up in the trees
where the green leaves are starting to sprout
with the buds of spring.
The shadows of the sun, look like frozen statues,
as there is only a slight breeze coming off the hills.
Among the crispness of the frost, daffodils are coming out
to see the world like a world of glittery frost.
In the depths of the ground, rabbits are still sleeping,
in hibernation from the winter, not trusting that winter is over.
Little lambs are being born and little bunnies too.
The sun comes out;
Ready for, another beautiful day.

Carolyn Dugon (14)
Whitchurch High School

WHAT IS AUTUMN?

Autumn is a butterfly,
Brightly coloured.
Brown, crimson, gold like patchwork
Booming off in the speckled southern sunset.

Autumn is a harsh wizard,
That casts a spell on the innocent trees,
Fizzing and hissing at the frail wildlife.

Autumn is a wanted crime,
On the loose, covered in guilt,
Covering the frightened air,
Breathing death amongst our clan.

Autumn is an unpopular outcast,
Chased away by the evil wind,
Washed along the lonely shore,
Left alone on an iced window ledge.

Jennifer Davidson (13)
Whitchurch High School

WINTER'S BEGINNING AND END

The sign is here,
The first drop of snow,
But there will be more,
Thousands more to go.

The desert of snow,
The land of white,
But nature unfortunately
Isn't winning this fight.

Only the strongest
Will survive this time,
Stay firm and green
And carry on their line.

But nature comes back
With a new beginning,
For after this harsh time,
Comes the turn for spring.

Antony Goodman (14)
Whitchurch High School

AROUND THE WORLD

Around the world in the velvety sky
lie thousands of stars shining up high,
Behind the world there is no life,
the stars are gone and so has the light,
In front of the world lies a magical kingdom,
the fantasies go beyond imagination.
On top of the world you have no worries,
you live with one another in tranquil harmony.
Under the world is a lost and dark city,
Destroyed.
Next to the world lies an extraordinary planet
like the Earth, but different in many ways.
Far from the world are millions of planets,
each one different in but all amazing.
In the centre of the world, there's no life at all,
the heat is sensational.
By the world are colourful gases dancing around
in the breeze.

Gemma Wilding (11)
Whitchurch High School

THE FIRST SMILE

See the girl with the smile on her face
The first ever smile
It slowly emerges
Like a fresh April shower
As she wears the smile
A beam of sun shines through the trees
It twinkles her smile
The first smile turns into the first laugh
A gentle sound that ripples the air
Like a splash of water in a crystal stream
The laugh is a bubble of joy
A bird flits through the sky
The laugh is great and loud
It echoes through the silence of the forest
A dark brown face and bright green eyes
Black hair streaming across her shoulders
See the girl with the laugh on her face
The first ever laugh
Why does the girl wear the smile?
What has caused her to laugh?
Was it the river that trickles softly?
Was it the forest that guards the creatures?
The girl is beautiful as she keeps the smile
Hidden in a secret place
In her heart the smile is kept
But on her face it is worn.

Rebecca Richards (12)
Whitchurch High School

THE SEASONS

Spring was here,
The sun was near.
The plants were growing
As the wind wasn't blowing.
Lambs were born
In the sunset at dawn.

Summer was here,
The sky was clear.
The fruits were being sold
At the price of gold.
The sun got higher,
It's as hot as fire.

Autumn was here,
Winter was near.
The autumn leaves were red,
The floor was like a red bed.
The nights got dark,
There were no squirrels seen in the park.

Winter was here,
There was a feeling of fear.
Snow started to fall,
Children had fun with lots of snowballs.
Christmas came round,
Presents were found.
These are the four seasons.

Sarah Francis (13)
Whitchurch High School

THE PARROT THAT LIVED IN BRAZIL

There was a parrot,
yellow and green.
It lived in Brazil
and was rarely seen.

It skimmed the trees
in the moonlight.
He ruffled his feathers
and said, 'Goodnight!'

The next day
in the gleaming sun,
He went for a fly
and got spun.

By a big, brown bird
who thought he was it.
But the parrot was gone,
he didn't like him one bit.

It happened again,
and twice more.
He saw his food,
and stretched out a claw.

The guy next door,
was red with fright,
He was so mad,
he put up a fight.

The parrot was shocked,
to see such a thing.
The parrot squealed
as he felt a sting.

The parrot dropped
from the sky,
I'm afraid to say
he had to die.

Laura Miles (11)
Whitchurch High School

THE WEREWOLF

A priest looks up into the black night,
The clouds drift across to reveal a secret,
A full moon,
The people won't sleep tonight.

Aaarrrggghhh! The werewolf shrieks,
His small hairy hands shake with fear,
His dark, meeting, evil-looking eyebrows ring with horror.
And now alas the werewolf roams the streets.

A werewolf's fur is as black as death,
The werewolf is death,
His stomach pines for human flesh,
He breathes his hot disgusting wet breath.

He is a cat,
The werewolf sees his prey,
He pounces, he kills silently and quickly,
The werewolf transforms and screeches like a bat.

The poor man sees what he's done and runs,
He hides,
Too ashamed to come out,
And now he is human again until the day is done.

Daniel Atkinson (12)
Whitchurch High School

AUTUMN

Summer was finished,
Fire and rust colours are a cloak
Over the fading sun,
Hiding away are woodland folk.

They fell secretly, softly,
Flitting through the air,
Rolling along pavements like waves of the sea,
Leaving trees bare.

Bare, no longer proud,
Trees stand shrivelled and brown, sharp and spiky;
Black house windows stare blankly at the trees,
They look evil not lively.

People rush around,
Dressed from head to toe
In layers and layers,
Or the cold wind will blow.

Soft blasts of wind,
Cold, a little harsh as they rush,
Brush on your cheek,
Brittle, crisp, causing a red blush.

It gets colder,
Could it be winter?
Violent, destructive and deadly,
Travelling through it goes Santa.

Gemma Collard (13)
Whitchurch High School

WINTER

The snow falls down onto my toes,
Bright red go my ears, cheeks and my nose.
My fingers are kept warm by my purple gloves,
While I'm making snowmen with the objects from above.
A quilt comes down and covers the land,
Still lovers are walking holding hand in hand.
Little red noses, ears and cheeks,
Are all you can see when you walk down the streets.
The trees are moulting and the flowers are hiding,
Every building has a white, silver lining.
Christmas is coming and everyone knows,
Soon Santa will be coming to good boys and girls.
The sun comes out and the snow starts to melt - spring is on its way,
The boys and girls are starting to cry,
It is another year until winter comes by.

Lauren Stacey (13)
Whitchurch High School

THE GARDEN

Around my garden live beautiful trees and flowers,
Behind the trees and flowers live creatures not known of,
Beside the creatures lives a sad, lonely figure.
On top of the lonely figure is a big, round hat.
Inside the hat lives another happy life,
In the happy life are happy people.
All the happy people have lollipops,
On all of the lollipops are holes,
Inside the holes are nothing at all.

Charles Moore (11)
Whitchurch High School

In The Summer When Ice Just Melts

The dawn chorus welcomes in the day,
Before you can see the sun's rays,
Children's play can be heard early in the morning,
While many people are still snoring.

The sun's rays beat down on the beach,
Where tourists are soaking their feet,
People can be seen eating ice-cream
Or sunbathing, having a nice dream,
Children are playing in the sand,
With their fathers lending them a hand.

In the night as you lay in bed,
You can see that the clouds have fled,
You have a clear view of the sky,
And you can still hear children being sly,
Barbecues can be smelt,
In the summer when ice just melts.

Samantha Kenealy (13)
Whitchurch High School

The Ocean

Behind the ocean are pirates, battling against life,
Above the ocean is a kite, gliding towards destiny.
Under the ocean lies a creeping monster, keeping a secret,
Beside the ocean waits the silent, golden snake,
                              following the tide,
Around the ocean lay floating islands, tired and drowsy.
Far from the ocean are children wishing for happiness.

Kate Holtam (12)
Whitchurch High School

KNOCK ON THE DOOR

Spirits are high
When summer rules
The sun is golden
Days shine like jewels
Until autumn knocks at the door
And summer is no more.

Leaves red
Fires ablaze
Birds fly afar
From the reclining haze
Until winter knocks at the door
And autumn is no more.

Icicles glint
From a bed of white
The cold wind howls
In the dead of night
Until spring knocks at the door
And winter is no more.

Young lambs leap
Yellow daffodils burn
We clearly rejoice
At the sun's return
Until summer knocks at the door
And spring is no more.

Jessica Robson-Davis (13)
Whitchurch High School

SPRING IS TAKING OVER

All the birds are coming back,
as the winter gets the sack.
Spring is taking over.

The snow and the ice are melting away,
Spring is chasing winter and keeping it at bay.
Spring is taking over.

All new animals are being born,
The warmer weather forces frogs to spawn.
Spring is taking over.

All the flowers are growing
and the farmers are sowing.
Spring has taken over now.

Rachel Booy (14)
Whitchurch High School

IN THE CLOUDS

On top of the clouds, I see a beautiful sky
with a bright, shining sun.
In the cloud, I see a black cloud
of thunder and rain.
Under the cloud, I see a beautiful,
paradise world.
To the left of the cloud, I see a flock
of birds flying towards me.
To the right, I see an aeroplane
polluting the skies.

Andrew Bridgeman (11)
Whitchurch High School

THE DOOR

Through the door is a hidden world
Of the future.
What will it bring?
Sadness, happiness, or a new life?

Next to the door hangs a painting
Which tells a story.
By the door is a gift of joy
Waiting to be unwrapped,
Around the door is an arch of roses
Protecting me.
But through the door is
A new life, an old life, your life,
My life.

Nia Edwards (11)
Whitchurch High School

THE GARDEN

In front of the garden, people sit in the hot sun laughing happily,
At the back of the garden, a secret wonderland is in the shadows,
Above the garden, the clouds float dreamily over the peaceful land
                              of bright flowers and happiness,
Then I wake up in a dark, dirty garden with spiders and other insects,
In the pitch-black night, cold.

Martha Kane (11)
Whitchurch High School

THE BUSH

Behind the bush is a small world of mystery,
Dotted with yellows, reds and greens.
Around the bush is an invisible boundary,
Trying to hide what it covers.
Inside the bush is a chamber of golden leaves,
Crispy, crumbly and bright.
Far from the bush is a howling, monstrous wind,
Trying to get to the bush,
But near the bush is the tinkling sound of a bird's morning song.
But all around the bush is one big problem which roams this earth.
This problem may seem quite complicated, but really it's not.
The problem is that too many monsters are polluting this earth.

Andrew Dyson (11)
Whitchurch High School

COOL CYMRU

Over the mellow, green mountains,
Through the rippling River Taff,
Under the grand gates of Caerphilly Castle,
Around Gabalfa Roundabout,
Inside the magnificent Millennium Stadium,
Where mighty crowds have roared.
Beside the great Aneurin Bevan statue,
A great man to behold,
Below the Severn Bridge, water rushes by,
This is my homeland and this is why every morning,
When I wake, I thank the Lord I'm Welsh.

Nicholas Shepherd (12)
Whitchurch High School

THE BLUE WEATHER REPORT

Hello and welcome to today's weather report;
The blue glassy sea is shimmering fiercely today as the blue sky above
is hanging like a bat suspended in mid-air.
As we go down into the middle part of town we see blue jelly beans
jumping up and down waiting to be bought.
There are people with blue jumpers on looking like blueberries walking
down the street heading in the direction of Whitchurch High School
today to make some blue sculptures (which will probably turn into
blobs) in art.
Oh and as we pass a house we see a dog with a blue collar on in a blue
kennel dancing around singing.
Now we come across the hospital. Grannies are coming out with blue
shawls on and babies with blue blankets are coming home, out of
hospital, to the big world (poor them).
Oh and the blue rain is just starting to pour down like blue cats and
dogs.

Thank you and tune in for tomorrow's forecast (red).
Good blue night.

Rachel Edwards (12)
Whitchurch High School

THE OCEAN

Beneath the ocean are happy memories, swimming through the sea,
Above the ocean is a paradise island, tranquil and desolate,
Below the ocean lives a world of joy,
Under the ocean is the dusty surface forgotten by the world,
Beneath the ocean swim creatures of the peaceful ocean,
Above the ocean is the sky, shrouded in cotton wool.

Laura Jones (12)
Whitchurch High School

THE TORNADO

It twists silently slithering slowly
Towards the ground getting faster,
Getting larger by the second,
Heading towards the town.
The town has no warning,
People are screaming as the twisting
Tornado sweeps through a paint factory,
The tornado turns green as the paint
Speeds around the tornado
Cars are crushed, crumpled by the power
Of the tornado.
After the tornado has gone, the town is trashed
And smashed.
The town has no standing buildings left
the whole town is smashed.
You can still taste the destruction
Small fires burning, crashed buildings,
the villagers hope this won't happen again.

Leon Daly (12)
Whitchurch High School

THE BEAST

Behind the beast's head lies an ocean, quite still,
In the middle of the beast's eyes lies a world of fright and fear,
Around the beast's head lies smoke and confusion,
Away from the beast's head lies an ocean, a paradise, a haven,
Above the beast's head lies darkness, nowhere to go,
The thing is dead.

Luke James (12)
Whitchurch High School

AUTUMN

Day is dawning,
Leaves are falling,
Animals are collecting food,
Soon it will be winter.

Winds are blowing,
Rivers flowing,
Days are getting shorter,
Soon it will be winter.

Hallowe'en is arriving,
Bonfires are starting,
Smoke's filling the air,
Soon it will be winter.

Nature is going to bed,
Trees are bare,
Nights are getting colder,
Soon it will be winter.

Matthew Richards (11)
Whitchurch High School

THE JAIL

Before the jail was built lived sadness and horror,
Through the jail lives anger and violence
Across the jail hallway you hear secrets which shouldn't be told,
Around the jail live worthless and lifeless people,
In front of the jail live peace and freedom.

Rhiannôn Clarke (11)
Whitchurch High School

THE OCEAN SEA

Up above lives a sky
full of creation, clouds shaped like animals.

Around the ocean live us
full of joy and happiness.

Below the ocean lives a different world
full of fish, lively as ever.

At the bottom of the ocean lies sand
still with seaweed overpowering it.

On top live white crashing waves
taking over the world beneath them.

At the end of the ocean the waves stop,
the sun reflects down onto the ocean sea.

Samantha James (11)
Whitchurch High School

THE MAGIC OF THE OCEAN

In the ocean swim fish that shimmer beneath the waves,
Above the ocean fly screeching seagulls hunting down their prey,
Near the ocean is a beach, waves gently lapping on the shore,
On the ocean sit tranquil boats, swaying calmly in the breeze,
Below the ocean lies a wreck, who knows what treasures it
may hold?
Beneath the ocean, I don't know, but there are dark secrets to
be told.

Laura Williams (11)
Whitchurch High School

FEELINGS

Feelings are like a group of angels
singing from the sky above.

Feelings are like a pair of scales,
once up then down.

Feelings are like a bad date,
always on your mind.

Feelings are like a Christmas tree,
bright and colourful

Feelings are like the weather,
always changing with every passing moment.

Kyle Smith (8)
Whitchurch High School

THE EARTH

In the earth is fiery lava,
Around the earth is a field of water,
On the earth are patches of green,
Above the earth is a dark blanket,
Sprinkled with glitter,
Walking the earth are millions of
Ant-like beings,
Lighting the earth is . . .
A ball of fire.

Matthew Edmonds (12)
Whitchurch High School

THE BEACH

As I walk along the crisp, golden sand
I stare out at the desolate sea,
Which seems to go on for ever.
The purple sun reflects beautifully,
Standing out against the pale sky.
I could feel the sand heating my feet
Like a warm, winter fire
And as ripples of water splashed up as far as my ankles,
I relaxed enjoying the ending of a perfect day.

Laura Diamond (12)
Whitchurch High School

THE WINDOW

Through the window is a perfect world,
Sun shining, people smiling.
Below the window lies rich, fertile land,
Covered in trees and flowers.
Above the window is a pale blue sky,
Filled with candyfloss clouds.
Around the window fly birds of all different sizes,
Chirping their cheery tune.
Behind the window stands me,
Looking out on my perfect world.

Jenny Donoghue (11)
Whitchurch High School

SUMMERTIME

The summer has come with its shining sun,
The children are laughing, having lots of fun,
The summer has come with the jumping waves,
People exploring the dark, empty caves.
The summer has come with its lush, green trees,
Mothers setting up picnics wave away the bees.
The summer has come with its ice-creams,
Daydreams and suncreams.
The summer has come and everyone's merry,
Jump in the car or hop on the ferry.
To the beach, to the beach,
Hear us all shout,
Summer is coming and we're going out.
Swimsuits and bathing caps,
Beach balls and cricket bats,
We're ready to go.
The weather is wonderful
The sun is so strong, its rays
Keep on beating for ever so long.
Not a breeze in the air,
The sea is so quiet, still, sweet and fair,
But alas, it is time for the day trip to end.
It's time to pack up all the bags and the balls
And head for the motorway, because home calls.
As I look behind from my back seat,
I can see the horizon and wavy foams of heat,
But I'm not sorry we're going, it's been a hard day,
Lazing about is really quite wearing.
Away home to my bed to get refreshed for the morning.

Kayleigh Llewellyn (13)
Whitchurch High School

THE SEA

Below the sparkling, foaming sea,
Lies a world of mystery.
Under rocks, pebbles, stones,
Are colourful fish and shells.
Over the sea jump huge great dolphins,
Making a show of their own.

Above the sea the white waves crash,
While slimy seaweed follows.
In the sea are gloomy shipwrecks,
Waiting to be found.
Over the sea the sunset waves,
To the distant land beyond.

Stephanie Bassett (11)
Whitchurch High School

OPEN UP

Behind the door lies distant memories,
In front of the door is a land of the future,
Around the door are problems encountered and solved,
Above the door are heavenly deeds,
Below the door are the bad times,
Open the door to wealth and happiness,
Open the door to a time of sadness,
Who knows? Open the door and find out.

Niall Allen (11)
Whitchurch High School

THE SEA

As the sea crashes and thunders
through the night,
It creeps towards the city,
The tide regains fish and crabs,
it left behind hours before.

The wind blows harder, the waves grow,
Ships and boats sway to and fro,
Clanging metal fills all ears,
until it decides to calm down.

When it calms the water goes still,
The sun clears the early mist,
And I can see for miles,
with no land in sight,
And I realise the sea is huge.

David Chick (11)
Whitchurch High School

THE SEA

Above the sea is a blue sky with cotton-like clouds,
Under the sea is a blue world of paradise.
Behind the sea is a beach with powdery white sand.
In front of the sea is a deserted beach with a rocky surface.
Around the sea are seagulls flying around
scavenging for food, any food
Which is rotten and worthless to us now.
The sea can change from a calm playful sea
to a rough sea which destroys ships
and takes people out so far that they can't swim back.

Daniel Mark Gardener (11)
Whitchurch High School

LAUGHTER

Laughter is a smile
on a small child's face

Laughter is like a stream
running through a valley

Cruel laughter is like someone
stabbing you in the back.

Cruel laughter is like breaking
a beautiful friendship.

Laughter is like Wales
winning the Rugby World Cup.

Emma Cousins (12)
Whitchurch High School

THE WINDMILL

There it stands in a field of its own
Waving its arms up in the air
Over here and over there.

It grinds the wheat until it's flour
to make it nice for hour after hour.

In the night the arms shall stop
as he drops asleep
in the cold and wintry night his
arms get frozen until tomorrow's light.

Rhys Cartwright (12)
Whitchurch High School

FEELINGS

Feelings are a bed of roses,
easily crushed and torn.

They are the sound of raindrops,
trickling down a stream.

They are leaves on a tree,
swaying with the wind.

They are fields and meadows,
with flowers brightly coloured.

They are the birds that fly high,
looking down at the ground.

They are knives with sharp blades,
that don't make a sound.

Hollie Uzzell (12)
Whitchurch High School

THE OCEAN

Above the ocean there are cotton wool balls in a blue crêpe paper sky,
Under the ocean lies a mysterious world and creatures unknown,
On top of the ocean the waves are crashing onto the rocky cliffs,
In the ocean swim brightly coloured and unusual fish,
Far across the ocean you can see small islands on the horizon,
Before the ocean lies a golden sandy beach,
Near the ocean are children happily splashing in the rockpools,
Below the ocean is a wreck of a ship with fish dancing in and out the
portholes.

Jodie Hollyman (11)
Whitchurch High School

A POEM ABOUT FEELINGS

They are flowers
In the sun.
Do not destroy.

They are china
Delicate and fragile.
Do not drop.

They are a saw
Can cut through you.
Be careful.

They are paper
Easily trampled on.
Watch out.

They are the sun
Makes you shine.
Feeling free.

Rebecca Pugh (13)
Whitchurch High School

THE MANEATER!

Lurking deep in the water.
Gliding, very slowly
Watching for the shadow,
Of his harmless prey.

His silver long body
His razor-sharp teeth.
His eyes are watching
For his harmless prey.

Splash! A surfboard overhead
His eyes fill with evil
His mouth starts to grin.
He approaches the surface.

It was a lucky escape,
The shark returns,
To his lonely place in the sea.

Vikki Richards (12)
Whitchurch High School

FRIENDS

They are money in a casino,
Can be won,
Can be lost.

Good friends are life,
You can't get rid of them.
Stick by you till the end.

They are vital organs,
You need them to survive.
Without them you are nothing.

They are confession boxes,
Someone to turn to.
Someone to share your secrets.

They aren't parasites,
They aren't vultures,
Or scavengers.

Leslie Nichols (12)
Whitchurch High School

LAUGHTER

Laughter is like a field of giggles,
a field of dreams,
a field of happiness
like a big pile of juicy sweets,
this always makes me happy.
Laughter can be like an insult
like something very hurtful.
Laughter is in two parts
a nice part and a horrible part.
The nice parts are like things that make you happy
as if you're abroad in the scorching sun.
The horrible part is mean.
It's nasty and horrible.
It's as if something you like disappears in an instant.
Now you've heard my opinion of laughter.
What's yours?
Laughter, laughter, laughter.
What does it make you think of
after reading my poem . . . ?

Donna Cartwright (12)
Whitchurch High School

FRIENDS

Friends are dogs,
walking with their
companions.

Friends are diamonds,
wrapped round a
lady's finger.

Friends are books,
read each page
carefully.

Friends are rainbows,
with bright colours
beaming.

Katie Taylor (12)
Whitchurch High School

LAUGHTER

Laughter is sweet
Sometimes sour
Sometimes sugar.

Laughter is words
They can hurt when or
if used incorrectly.

Laughter is friends
A caring hug or
a spiteful tongue.

Laughter is dogs
Playing kindly or
A vicious growl.

Laughter is diseases
Sometimes cured
Sometimes not.

Sarah Madley (12)
Whitchurch High School

THE MONSTER

It was dark,
as dark as a witch's heart,
I looked around,
Then I saw him,
Standing there, in front of me,
Staring with his cold blue eyes.
His skin, purple with yellow lumps.
It was quiet.
Then, I heard loud bumps.
He's coming after me,
He's getting closer and closer,
He's still staring at me
Longing for me to be his meal
but then . . .

I woke up!

Grant Pearcy (12)
Whitchurch High School

SEASIDE FUN!

Not far from here, there's a lovely beach,
Filled with children, all with sandy feet.
Sandcastles, sandcastles everywhere,
Madness has struck, no time to spare.

The sound of the ice-cream van and everyone runs,
Shouting and screaming, all children having fun,
Splish, splash, the sound of the waves,
Soaking the sandcastles that have just been made.

The sparkling water, the gleaming sun,
And of course ice-creams, yum, yum, yum!
All those boats that just sail past,
And the donkey rides, I wish they'd go fast.

The sun's almost setting, it's not very light,
People are leaving, that can't be right,
But still, the seaside's so great, it'll make you run,
So you better hurry, if you want to have fun!

Natasha Patel (11)
Whitchurch High School

THE MYSTERIOUS CAT

Its ears are as shiny as glitter,
Its nose is as wet as a damp cloth,
Its paws are as soft as velvet,
Its teeth are as sharp as thorns,
It's a mysterious cat!

Its ears are as pointed as daggers,
Its whiskers are as thin as wire,
Its tail is like a whip that lashes out,
Its fur is as smooth as silk,
It's a mysterious cat!

It purrs as it sleeps,
It eats like a vacuum cleaner,
It plays like crazy,
It is very young but
It's a mysterious cat!

James Price (12)
Whitchurch High School

FRIENDS

They are precious gems,
diamonds, rubies, emeralds and sapphires.

They are mothers,
picking you up,
when you're down.

They are your favourite football team,
winning the Premiership.

They are walking through
a pretty meadow,
on a cool calm day.

They are chocolate ice-cream,
with chocolate sprinkles.

They are a theme park,
with lots of different,
exciting rides.

They are getting rid
of your favourite pet.

Hirra Ahmad (12)
Whitchurch High School

THAT'S WHY I LIKE CATS

Cats are just like baby tigers
They sleep around all day long
But they liven up in the night
Chasing things and having fights
That's why I like cats.

Cats are very, very nice
But all they like is chasing mice
Cats howl and prowl all day long
It is just like they are singing a song
That's why I like cats.

Jade Ashment (12)
Whitchurch High School

FEELINGS

Feelings are elevators,
People can ride you high,
Or they can take you down,
Simply with the touch of a button.

Feelings are flying kites,
Soaring in the sky,
When there is no wind to boost you,
You'll be sailing to the ground.

Feelings are matchstick houses,
Very pleasing when up,
Be careful with them,
They'll easily crumble.

Feelings are dynamite,
They can be so small,
When lit.
They do great damage.

Feelings are ladders,
Climb them high with compliments,
But if you slip,
You'll be tumbling down.

Paul Workman (12)
Whitchurch High School

THE GARDEN

There is a place I often like to go,
and to you I will now show.
My place where I like to be,
is here behind the chestnut tree.

My garden sparkles with long-stemmed roses,
to which one are light and delicate like clouds.
Their whiteness, it is quite petite,
so white like a fresh clean sheet.

The fruit is my orange tree,
are nice and sweet just like me.
The daffodils are as golden as the sun,
and the bees collect nectar from everyone.

A fountain squirts water all over the ground,
and the grass soft as satin doesn't utter a word.
The ivy climbs up the granite walls,
it leaves none showing and covers all.

As I leave this wonderful place,
my heart doesn't fill with heartache.
It doesn't fill itself with sorrow,
as I know I will be back tomorrow.

Andrew Thomas (12)
Whitchurch High School

THE DOVE

Gliding silently through the night
A bright dazzling white
Singing sweet melodies
There's heartache with agony
For remorseful listeners unlucky in love.

Perching modestly on a spray of emerald green
Gracefully preening his glossy sheen
He glances down at the accessible
Admiring people
And, cocking his head, wonders what brought him
To be the dove.

Laura Cowley (12)
Whitchurch High School

WHAT IS A FRIEND?

What is a friend?
Is it someone who is rich?
Is it someone who is poor?

Is it someone who helps you?
Is it someone who does not help you?

What is a friend?
Is it someone who knows what to say?
Is it someone who is lost for words?

Is it someone who shares sandwiches with you?
Is it someone who would not share chocolate with you?

Maybe a friend is imaginative when you are lonely,
My friend is caring, sharing and she understands me.

My friend is always there for me,
My friend is like a sister to me.

My friend is for life,
She is my sister and my best friend.

Katie Bennett (12)
Whitchurch High School

LOCH NESS

They wonder what it is they see,
A whale, croc,
Or even a submarine.
For years they wonder,
Without a clue,
Within the murky,
muddy loch,
Something lurks beneath the sea,
People have pictures,
And tapes,
But they all go wrong,
For that is a mystery,
For what they see is a wonder,
A prehistoric survivor.
A giant fish 12 metres long,
10,000 sightings of the fish,
it's a wonder,
because only 3,000,
have been recorded,
But people say it is a ghost,
so they sent a priest,
to exorcise a ghost.
Is that all they're seeing?
A ghost?
Would it have worked?
Is that what they are all seeing?
A ghost?
Is that why the sightings have gone wrong?
You tell me.

Bradley David (13)
Whitchurch High School

THE BEACH

The great white horses crash upon the beach
With the crystal blue sea behind them.
From across the bay and
Over the rocks, the sea drowns the beach.

On the beach, the sea has taken over
The people have gone.
On the beach the fishes have taken their places.
Over the cliff all you can see is sparkling blue.
Under the sea the fishes swim.

Everything is now still
All the great white horses
Have died.
The sea is forever silent.

Matthew Popek (11)
Whitchurch High School

MYSTERIES OF THE MIND

Beside this mind lies a land of wonderful mysteries being
                                        carried to happiness,
In this mind lies red sun, setting in the world of dreams,
Far from this mind lies sky as blue as heaven shimmering like a gem,
Back of this mind lies poverty and destruction depressing souls,
Past this mind lies heartbroken tales upsetting dull and empty heads,
Into this mind lies thoughts and dreams which no one knows!

Charlotte McCormack (11)
Whitchurch High School

THE OCEAN

Beneath the sea is like an army of soldiers
Marching courageously going to battle.
At the bottom of the sea is a ship
Being torn away by the sea.
On top of the sea are waves like
A herd of elephants.

Above the sky is a big empty space
Like a room with nothing inside.
Before the open space are clouds
Like puffs of smoke drifting through
Bitter wind that cuts away at the shapes.

A crowded ship moving on top of the fast ocean
And birds flying over like flapping hands.
Sunbeam rulers come down from a yellow tennis ball
To stitch them all together.

Andrew Davis (11)
Whitchurch High School

WINTER BLUES

The chilling winter wind is whistling
Howling through the trees like a child's cry.
Winter is a harsh black knight,
Marching forward, freezing all in sight.
It charges, swallowing up the light,
All the ground freezes overnight.
Slowly spring arrives with all its might,
And winter has finally lost the fight.

Thomas Marchant (14)
Whitchurch High School

THE STRONG WIND

Besides the wind is an animal or a chair.
Between the wind is a dangerous black hole.
In front of the wind is the blue drifting water.
Below the wind is the deep end.

The green and blue wind.
The wind as strong as thunder blowing everything away, the towns,
the cities.
The roofs are pulling off the houses like paper coming off a paper clip.

The movements of a delicately strong wind.
Are like movements of a pin.
The cleverness of the wind is like a calculator multiplying
and subtracting
The people call it a hurricane!

Aisha Khan (11)
Whitchurch High School

THE SEA

Above the sea is a majestic, magical land,
Where the four seasons cast their spells,
Where the summer angels dance in joy,
Beneath the clear blue cloudless sky,
Below the sea is a quiet, mysterious, seabed,
Where the sea animals swim peacefully,
On the sea is where the sun reflects gently,
Where the glistening light is brighter than ever,
At the seashore is the place to be,
Where the perfect land meets the perfect sea.

Rachael Jones (11)
Whitchurch High School

HAPPY

There's a sunflower outside
It looks like it's touching the clouds
The day is very bright
The children are shouting out loud.

I'm up in my room
It's big with bright green walls
I wish I was on the beach
Playing volleyball.

I'm lying on my bed
There's noises in my head
It feels like I'm having a dream
Then I start to scream
Then I wake up and realise
It's just a dream.

When I look at the sunflower
My smile starts to beam
I start to feel like it's looking at me.

So I go downstairs
And I sit and stare
There's nobody there
Except me and the yellow sunflower
Which is way up there.

Kelly Curtis (12)
Whitchurch High School

A Change Of Scene

Monkeys swing from tree to tree
Fish swim in a clear blue sea
I listen to the flowers, they seem to hum
There's a fiery sky and a big red sun
The refreshing smell of lemons waft through the air
Glitter falls from the clouds into my hair
Sand on the beach is soft and warm
The meadows are filled with golden corn
All of a sudden there is a riot
As quick as a flash, it's totally quiet
I soon realise that devastation's come
The flowers, they no longer hum
The fiery sky is now not there
A smoky smell runs through the air
I'm falling through a pool of mist
Everything by death has been kissed
A rainbow runs right through the sky
I can see colour in the corner of my eye
I then lie down and go to sleep
On a bed of wool from a purple sheep
I'm sure I can hear my mother's voice
To open my eyes I have no choice
For some reason I see the walls of my room
I knew this dream would end too soon.

Danielle Burke (12)
Whitchurch High School

TRAPPED

Inside your world it's a sea of tears,
Faint laughing can be heard,
Sharp rocks are below so you mustn't fall,
The smell of sadness surrounds you,
Above you is the reflection of the moon,
There is no escape, you're trapped.

Inside your small, narrow room,
There is a small window with bars,
The walls are black with streaky lines,
There is no one,
You are alone,
In the corner there's a small, white wooden chair,
There is a door,
It is locked,
There is no escape, you're trapped.

Inside your room, you'll find a plant,
It is tangled creeping ivy,
It is dark and envious,
It winds itself around you,
Choking you,
There is no escape, you're trapped.

Louisa Bird (12)
Whitchurch High School

NATURE

Flowers falling, roses are dying, trees are
bending, grass is changing, lights are dark,
Bright colours are dark, dark as purple.
Everyone's miserable, miserable as nature,
It's awful.

Nine o'clock in the morning, spring is near,
flowers are growing, roses are rising,
trees are up, grasses are green, lights are bright,
Dark colours are bright, bright as blue.
Everything's alive! Nature's back.

Shima Begum (11)
Whitchurch High School

AUTUMN GALE

As we wait in the long, tiring traffic jam,
We begin to hear a rumble,
Not of a car, not of a train, but of the wind.
The car begins to sway,
Back and fore,
Back and fore,
Then bang!
Something hits the car,
As I turn around to look,
I see hundreds of leaves and branches,
Still moving in the wind.
The leaves rustle as though they are waving at us
Through the rear window,
The wind dies down,
The traffic clears,
The car moves slowly forward,
The branches slide off gracefully,
Leaving nothing behind but a few dents.

Philip Cole (11)
Whitchurch High School

A POEM ABOUT MY FRIEND RACHEL

My friend Rachel
likes to eat sweets
when she's with me that's all she eats!

My friend Rachel
likes to eat pasta
she just can't eat it any faster!

My friend Rachel
likes to eat chips.
That's all you see
go through her lips!

But these are the reasons she is my friend
though she drives me round the bend!

Lucie Deacon (12)
Whitchurch High School

BOREDOM

There are miles of dead countryside,
There are bones scattered in the dust,
There is a patch of sand, it is blowing in my eyes,
There is a little house,
I find myself in a small room with no windows,
There is no door, the only light is a small hole in the roof,
There is a little weed coming from a crack in the corner of the wall,
The walls are grey.
I am bored!

Andrew Edwards (12)
Whitchurch High School

HAPPINESS

When I think of happiness
it makes me tingle inside
I dream of being in Oakwood
on my favourite ride

I think of my favourite colours
blue, yellow and red
I think of my favourite uncle
his name is Uncle Ted
when I am asleep dreaming in my bed
I dream of being in the clouds
peering down at the world ahead
I dream of being a bird
flying straight ahead.

Steven Groves (12)
Whitchurch High School

THE COUNTRYSIDE

The countryside, like a window to life.
The cornfields swaying in the wind.
The trees like knights of old,
Protecting their territory from intruders.
A small sparrow darting overhead.
The countryside, so peaceful,
No cars or buses or the hustle and bustle of the city.
The countryside, like a window to life.
No overhead cables or phone lines messing up the sky.
The countryside, so peaceful.

Gareth John Knowles (12)
Whitchurch High School

DEPRESSED

I am in a room,
Nothing in there,
But the bad things in my life,
Playing with my mind.

I see a plant, it's a rose,
Someone gave me that rose,
It's now dead, lifeless and colourless
All the petals on the floor.

I am in a hot place,
Nothing to the north, south, east or west,
I see a lizard walk by in my shade,
The only shade is my shadow and the
Cracks in the dusty surface.

Luke Merrey (12)
Whitchurch High School

SUMMER

The sun arose with an orangey glow,
Looking upon a farmer who's starting to sow.
He is coloured as red as a rose,
His gentle warmth shines as the cockerel crows.
He is so lazy, he makes you feel,
That he's dressed in a giant orange peel.
The sheep are happy chewing the grass,
The sun is descending rather fast.
The sun disappears over the hill,
Leaving the people with a springy chill.

Richard Smith (13)
Whitchurch High School

BORED

Small, dark, black, no windows
Narrow, not much air
The walls are black
No furniture
No noise
No one else in the room apart from me

My plant is dead,
All the leaves are brown and falling off
It's about two foot tall and very thin
It's leaning on its side.

The grass is dead and there is no life anywhere
Thundery clouds mass in the dark sky
It's cold and smells like rotten eggs
In the distance there is an abandoned cottage
The windows are smashed.

Ian Richards (12)
Whitchurch High School

CITIES!

C ar horns beeping and honking,
I   n a traffic jam of cars, moving like snails!
T raffic lights changing colours as people cross roads,
I   nfants crying, adults chatting, going to and from shops,
E veryone choking as factory fumes fill the air,
S kyscrapers towering above us, in our concrete world.

Lea Evans (11)
Whitchurch High School

THE EARTH

The world has land
The land is green
It can always look
Very mean
The Earth has water
The water is blue
There are lots of things
That people do
In the big, round world
Where we live
This is what we give
To community
To pollution
To wildlife too
Do we cause pollution?
Do you think we do?

Lacey Hinton (13)
Whitchurch High School

RED

The hatred of everything,
The swirling blood,
Your heart beating a thousand times.
The exciting thrill of fire and danger,
Hatred and evil destroying our lives,
Every minute of the day.

Jack Bird (12)
Whitchurch High School

HIGH ON HAPPINESS

I am on the moon,
In a square room with a large window,
The sun is shining brightly.
The room is cosy.
At the back of the room there is a sofa,
It is bright sky blue.
In the corner of the room there is a happy plant,
It is full of laughter and smiles.
Outside music is playing,
And people are bouncing but not because of the gravity,
But because of them being high on happiness.

Andrew Roberts (12)
Whitchurch High School

THE HURRICANE

Hurricanes, the heart of death and destruction,
Ripping turf to smithereens.
From countryside to cities
There is mayhem and panicking.
Slates breaking, windows smashing,
Trees swaying, cars flying,
Roads destroyed, debris everywhere.
When will it stop? Nobody knows,
Is this the worst hurricane yet?
Will there be more to come?

James Huntington (13)
Whitchurch High School

DEPRESSION'S WORLD

I'm in a room,
A room of deep gloom
Confined and blackened
No windows, no doors
No light, no warmth.
Just me.
Me and my sorrows.
On a hard declining chair
I see nothing but sadness
I feel trapped
I cannot escape
From this isolated gloom.

I'm a weed
Shrivelled and worn
Depressed and isolated
Deeply saddened
Saddened deeply
Reduced to shrivels
A bottomless pit
My leaves are deteriorated
Scrumpled
Reaching ever lower
Ever sinking into the soil.

The derelict, deteriorating landscapes
Torn down skyscrapers
Cloudy skies
Gloomy blackened
A role of thunder
A creak of lightning

Waterfalls of rain
Muddy polluted rivers
Stagnant waters
Dead trees, dead fields
I feel depressed
All the world's a crater
And all the people are mere weeds.

Aneka Jugessur (12)
Whitchurch High School

NATURAL COLOURS

Beautiful colours: reds, greens and yellows,
On trees, flowers and bushes.
The deep, dark yellow shade on the sun,
With a fiery feeling,
Pleasant and warm.

Red on the sun,
A warm, fiery shade
With yellow glowing beams,
Beaming down on a lush, green field,
Burning the backs of the cattle and sheep.

Green, green fields, lush and ripe.
Strawberries ripening and flowers blooming,
The sheep dog barking to the farmer shouting,
The sheep terrified as the dog flocks them in,
The farmer's wife calling,
'Dinner's ready darling!'

Greg Smith (13)
Whitchurch High School

BOREDOM STRIKES

I'm bored, I can't find anything to do.
I am in a room,
Which is small and dark,
I feel like I'm suffocating,
I can't see outside, there are no windows,
I try to scream but no one will hear,
I can't escape, I feel trapped,
As I stare at the bare walls I can see red bows edged with black,
There is no noise,
Everything is silent,
Nobody moves,
I'm being tortured by isolation.

I'm bored, I can't find anything to do,
I see a plant,
Which is a weed,
It's dark green face looks at me and says 'Please Miss, spare me
Find me a way out of the room,'
If you leave it alone it will grow and grow,
Its dry leaves are big and cover the dandelions.

I'm bored, I can't find anything to do,
I am in a small lane,
That is pitch-black dark,
And cramped for space,
It's long and dark and full of spiders,
It's surrounded by fields with dead flowers and rubbish.
I can smell burning and smoke,
The sky is black and gloomy,
As I look at the sky it looks like it's going to thunder,
There's no one around,
And all I can hear are the trees being blown around by the wind.

Kirsty Wilsher (12)
Whitchurch High School

HAPPINESS PLUS

Bright purple and green and orange in colour,
Compared to no room can it be said duller,
Full of life and satisfaction,
The room itself the size of a mansion,
At day and at night a good time is had,
Come to this house and you will be glad,
This beautiful plant is short of no love,
Shone on and cried on from the skies above,
As it brings new life it grows even more,
And its roots will continue right down to Earth's core,
It's young shall replace it when it sadly dies,
But shall carry its spirit right up to the skies,
This place that these two things so elegantly lie,
Is so full of life, there's no reason to cry,
How can this be such a wonderful place?
It's all down to us people of the human race.
It is so important, belonging to us,
Is made by the emotion of happiness plus.

Gareth Delve (12)
Whitchurch High School

FEELINGS

I cannot scream, I am so scared, my eyes have frozen
I feel so scared and frightened, my eyes went blue.
I am so angry, I grind my teeth until they are white
I throw food and china, my whole face goes bright red.
I feel anger in my eyes
I just want to go *pop!*

Beejan Shirvani (11)
Whitchurch High School

THE SPIRAL OF TERROR

Destruction is upon us.
There is fear in the air.
The hurricane is coming,
To destroy our welfare.

You are never safe.
It whirls and roars,
Just like a ravenous beast,
Destroying everything in sight
            with razor-sharp claws.

The eye of the storm passes over,
Harmony is regained.
Until it leaves us,
When chaos is back again.

The hurricane has gone now,
Safety has returned.
Although we are safe now,
It is though our lives have been burned.

Richard Duffy (12)
Whitchurch High School

BLUE

Blue is the colour of the sea,
Refreshing you on a hot, summer's day.
It's also cool and laid back,
It's also the colour of the sky.
But it's not just one colour,
Light by day, dark by night.

Simon Stephens (12)
Whitchurch High School

FEELINGS OF LIFE

You are on your own sad and lonely.
You're empty inside.
Your heart is longing.
Tears force themselves from your eyes.
Coldness falls around you like a cloud
What a lonely heart.

Jealousy pulls at your bones.
Having so much but wanting more.
A little voice inside saying, 'I want it !'
Corrupting your insides.
What a jealous mind.

Anger burning inside you.
You want to scream but no sound emerges.
Immortal power floods to your brain.
All your eyes can see is red.
What an angry cry.

Do not deny the emotions I speak of.
Learn to use them wisely.
Anger will always be inside you waiting to come out.
Jealousy will always be the pull of your heart.
Learn to live with loneliness but don't keep it
                              locked up inside.

Amber Thomas (11)
Whitchurch High School

FEELINGS

When I'm happy I'm warm and free,
When I'm angry I put dog food in someone else's tea.
When I'm lonely I'm hungry and sad,
When I'm furious I'm raging mad.
When I'm hungry I have a hot pie,
When I'm embarrassed I'm red like fire.
When I'm left out, to join in is my desire.
When I'm frightened I'm scared and afraid,
When I'm very happy I'm being paid.
When I'm excited I wish I could fly,
When I'm sad I cry and cry.
When I'm wondering I say, 'Why oh why?'
When I'm enjoying myself the days go by and by.
When I'm mad I'm such a liar,
When I'm helpful, I help fix a tyre.
When I'm bored I watch telly,
When I'm full, I have a bad belly.

Sarah Roberts (11)
Whitchurch High School

BLACK

The day is drowned by the evil
of night's darkness,
The stench of darkness lurks in the
smothering, pain-filled air.
The fear of illness loiters around every
awaiting corner of life.
But black is, and always will be part
of the never-ending circle of life.

Kimberley Shellard (12)
Whitchurch High School

TORNADO

I am a whirling, towering monstrosity
I can move anything large or small
I am dark
I am evil and cruel
I strike fear in all those with sense
I am destruction
I destroy all that is in my way
I wrestle my way through town and country
I am a murderous swine
I am terror from the heart of the Earth
I cause pain and suffering
I enjoy pain and suffering
I love destitution
I kill for pleasure and fun
I cut down the population of my victim town
I find people out, you can't hide
I am a tornado
I am death.

Thomas Baker (12)
Whitchurch High School

TURQUOISE

The peaceful, but magical,
Colour turquoise.
Unicorns, fairies and wizards,
Turquoise dragons with pink spots,
They're not breathing fire, but water!
Fantasies that mystify,
Our mystical friend turquoise.

Heather Williams (12)
Whitchurch High School

FIRE, FIRE

I saw a fire in my eyes,
the flames were dancing round me,
I saw a bonfire spitting sparks,
lighting up the sky,
with blue, yellow, red and orange,
darting with life in the evening sky.

I saw a fire burning, reflecting in your eyes.
The flames were dancing round you,
like lightning in the sky,
glimmering lights in time.

Fire, fire burning bright
like heat in the evening light.
Warning the world with your golden light.

Samantha Haines (12)
Whitchurch High School

RED

Red is the colour of our Welsh dragon,
The red dragon is the sign for our Welsh players.
Red also stands for Cupid the one who shoots
arrows to make people fall in love.
Red is the sign of danger,
Red stands for fire,
Red also stands for the red devil.

Donna-Marie Taylor (12)
Whitchurch High School

SHARK

I swam along the warm, blue sea
The sea went darker and darker
The waves were getting bigger and bigger
I shouted, 'Shark, shark,'
There was lots of screaming around me
Everybody swam as fast as they could
'Shark, shark,' they shouted
I was very, very cold
'I can't see the shark' I shouted
I swam as fast as I could
He's got my foot
I pulled my foot
I shout for help
Oh no he's got me.

Stacey Green (12)
Whitchurch High School

FUTURE VOICES POEM

In the future I want to see world peace,
For all wars and battles to stop and cease.

I want animal cruelty to come to an end,
For poachers to see what it's like to be penned.

I want doctors to make all diseased patients cured,
For illnesses like AIDS not to be pushed aside or ignored.

I want all evil to end, for a world without crime,
These things I see happening in the future, in time!

Sian Evans (13)
Whitchurch High School

AIRLESS

Empty, void blows hot and cold
I look around
The lady has vanished into thin air.

The mist brings out the spirits
The clouds bring out the rain
The sky brings out the heavens
I turn around and she's gone again.

Limp and lifeless plants are dying
Children, men and women are crying
Lack of air, no balloons are flying,
An alien falls from the sky.
She's gone again, I wither and die.

Zak Hussain (12)
Whitchurch High School

BLUE

When I am down death is near,
Death is cold and blue,
The sky is not the blue I am used to,
The sea is cold, uncaring water,
A carpet of blue gloom,
High treacherous waves,
The waves of fear,
The bullies know what they do,
It's so unfair and no one cares,
When I am down I think things through,
I ask myself what's best to do.

Colette Maggs (12)
Whitchurch High School

SCHOOL LIFE

Isn't school a drag?
Going to school every day,
Always on time,
Always in their special way.

Why are school uniforms so tacky?
They always make me itch!
The blue is supposed to make you smarter.
Well the hell with that I say.

The toilets always smell of smoke,
In every sort of way.
We hardly ever get in there
Because they're vandalised every day.

The leftover garbage stinks,
It smells like icky poo.
But it tells me one thing,
I won't be in school very soon.

But it's the loneliness that gets me most,
I'm lonely every day.
The loneliness is something very harsh,
Because I have no one with whom to play.

Paul Fletcher (13)
Whitchurch High School

SPACE

The moon twinkles on an empty world
Giving light to the Earth below.
The children asleep,
The adults downstairs,
But the moon still shines on through.

Some people look at his smiley face
He winks a wink to them.
He hears a rocket, a shooting star
Or even a meteor.

A spaceman jumps on his dusty face,
Leaving his steps to show.
He never stops,
He never stays
Just places another flag.

The rocket leaves
The spaceman goes and leaves this
world alone.
It returns to quiet, empty and still
But never away from home.

Alun James Thomas (11)
Whitchurch High School

THE TIGER

So secret at first
Rustling through the jungle grass
It spots its prey
Swiftly, closer it gets
Then a roar like thunder
A pounce so mighty.

Onto the unsuspecting victim
Silence claims the jungle
Its soft, striped fur spotted with blood
It leaves nothing left
So secret at first
To claim another life.

Eleanor Dearden (11)
Whitchurch High School

LESSONS!

The lessons I love,
the lessons I hate,

> Either one,
> I can talk to a mate.

But not all the time,
because I still have to learn,

> I realise now how important it is,
> I just have to be firm.

The work I do should always
be neat,

> And on a test
> I should never cheat.

I should always work
hard to get good grades,

> My concentration and effort
> should never fade.

The homework I get
is not just for fun,

> And if I don't do it
> I will get detention!

Emily Lawrence (13)
Whitchurch High School

BORED!

Another boring day at school,
With lessons that I hate,
You have to listen in school
They make you concentrate.
First we have assembly
Then we have break,
Then I have HE
But I'll just decorate.
But now at this moment
That I feel every day
That I'm just trying to stay
Awake.
The time is here 3:45
The bell rings and I run for my life.

Sophie Janine Cavan (13)
Whitchurch High School

SHARK

It moves swiftly through the sea
like the beast of the bluest ocean.
It can grow to 30 metres long,
It will eat anything in its way,
Its thick skin reflects beautifully on the sun,
It scares anything in its path,
It roams the sea like it owns it,
It makes quiet, bubbly sounds and as for his
big, beady eyes you could miss them but
it will sniff you out miles away.

Stephen Popple (11)
Whitchurch High School

SEASIDE FUN!

Seagulls flying overhead,
People out on their surfboards
Lapping and catching the waves,
As the ice-cream van arrives, the children run.

At the top of the sandy beach,
A row of shops
Displaying outside their varied range
Of buckets and spades.

That is where all the children are heading,
As the ice-cream van approaches,
The children scream and shout,
They run about getting money.

People in the sea having a good time,
Swimming with their rubber-rings,
And lilos big and small,
Some of the smaller children wearing armbands.

Flip-flop, flip-flop,
Go the feet of the people walking along the edge of the sea,
Taking a stroll,
Watching the speedboats and the occasional jet ski fly by.

Sandcastles made near and far,
Some with flags,
Others getting their photo taken,
Others getting destroyed by the violent waves.

Charlie Welch (11)
Whitchurch High School

THE CORRIDOR

Push and pull,
The bell has rung,
People pack up.
Then they jam through the door,
Teachers shouting don't,
You get into line.

Push and pull
They run down the corridors.
Year 7s go flying
Breaking legs and arms
The shouting of the children
Breaks the windows.

Push and pull
The traffic has gone,
A squad of teachers go out
Wall display on the floor.
The teachers pick up the children
And the wall displays,
Then they wait for the next lesson,
For the havoc again.

Simon Ward (14)
Whitchurch High School

TIMETABLE

The bell rings - it's 9.00am
Where to go? Room 99
What's Miss talking about?

The bell rings - it's 12.30pm
Where to go? Canteen for lunch
How much are the foods?

The bell rings - it's 1.30pm
Where to go? Room 30
What are all the lessons for?

The bell rings, it's 3.45pm
Where to go? Outside school
That's the beginning of my day.

Enoch Ho (13)
Whitchurch High School

TEACHERS

There is a teacher,
A very nice teacher,
She lets us speak in class,
She lets us eat in class,
With this teacher we don't do any work.

There is a biology teacher,
She's not very nice,
She shouts like a banshee,
She laughs like a witch,
With this teacher we do lots of work.

There is a head teacher,
He's tall and bald,
He gives out letters of dismay,
He thinks he's big (he is),
But anyone could have him in a fight.
With the head we behave.

As you can tell,
I don't like many teachers,
But school is *the best days of your life!*

Christopher Lucas (13)
Whitchurch High School

SCHOOL

School is like a prison but only goes on for six hours a day
Endless classes which go on and on each day
Teachers treat us like pets
We just copy, copy, copy
Some kids spoil classes and we don't get anything done.
Some kids are really nice and really try hard
School I hate, we should debate on why we have it.
I sometimes like school, especially when Wales play
School's quite fun after a year
Especially when you are clear
Homework isn't hard and we hardly get any
School is just a maze to me.

Bill Davis (13)
Whitchurch High School

SCIENCE

Oh I like science
And it's my favourite subject,
I'm in top set
And any messing around,
They are the reject!

Chemicals, burners, liquids alike
But I don't care
Because that's what I like.
But gas is what I don't like,
The smell is like a stinky spike.

But science is science,
And I like it.

Mark A Sweeney (13)
Whitchurch High School

A St Bernard Dog

I'm fat, yet fit,
Large, yet cute,
Very cold, yet panting,
I snore like a pig,
And grunt like a hog.
I'm as loyal as a friend
And I am a true friend.
I'm neither Barry,
Nor Beethoven,
But I look like them.
I rescue people in the snow,
I pant, even though I drink,
I wallow in mud,
But am as clean as soap,
I swim and eat,
But am as soft as a pillow!

Geraint Huw Denison (11)
Whitchurch High School

Light Pink

A fluffy marshmallow floating in the air,
Flying horses in heaven,
Angel Delight on a hot summer's day,
Cupid setting his arrow on a cute boy,
                    Pink.

Catherine Ashley (12)
Whitchurch High School

AIR

He slivers around the spacious room,
Elusive to the human eye.
He is hard to touch and is hard to see,
All you can feel is his cold breeze.
It gives you the goosebumps,
He can never be caught,
No one can keep up with his speed,
And even when they do
He vanishes into little cracks.
You can only feel his cold breeze
Which whispers around the room,
So when you feel that cold breeze in that
                                        spacious room,
Just look, he is nowhere to be seen.

Liam Scott (12)
Whitchurch High School

SPRING

She appeared from nowhere,
But spring was there,
A saviour from winter's cruel snare.

With her came
The sun and the rain,
Releasing life into the land again.

The birds sang to tell of her coming,
Buds did start appearing,
And all of a sudden there was a flurry of colour,
For the flowers had started to bloom.

Jessica Heaton (13)
Whitchurch High School

MOTHER NATURE

The skyscrapers wither in Mother Nature's hands,
Hailstones fall like golf balls,
Smashing and destroying everything in their path,
The thunder booms and deafens everyone around,
Then they see it,
The tornado is heading straight for them,
With its invincible, mind blowing effects, it deforms and kills
          everything near it
By hurling it hundreds of feet in the air,
The city centre, motorways, roads and houses are all silent,
There are no people around,
Because everyone knows the severe consequences and after effects.

Adam Shields (13)
Whitchurch High School

SURFING

It's a nice, sunny day at the beach
when a big wave hits your board.
You're dancing through the waves
like a bullet.
Huge waves and water splashing
across your face.
All of a sudden you fall off your board,
then you start floating across the water
like a fish.
Then all of a sudden you speed to
the water's edge,
by a wave hitting you.
What am I doing?

Ben Taylor (12)
Whitchurch High School

THE SEASIDE

To the beach we go,
Moving swiftly down the motorway, until the slow, winding road.
Up the steps out on the cliff,
Boats out on the water sail over the horizon.

We swim in cold, salty waters,
We play cricket at a slow tempo,
We laze around reading novels,
We build large, detailed sandcastles.

We eat sandy, dried out sandwiches,
We eat ready *sanded* crisps,
Ice lollies melt into drinks,
Apple cores get buried in the sandy beach.

We sail around the island of Caldy,
The seals look like great, wet pebbles,
We browse around the shops,
The rock shop is littered with feet lollies, fudge and fried eggs.

We buy our supper of pizza and chips
To eat on the way home,
It's sad to leave but we are so very tired,
From the beach we go.

Arthur Duncan-Jones (11)
Whitchurch High School

WHITE

The fluffy, white clouds filled with snow,
The freezing cold wind tickling my nose,
The clouds slowly moving across the sky
like an angel flying high.

Ben M Brown (12)
Whitchurch High School

SCHOOL

School is full of many surprises
especially when the teacher arises.
She may tower
but never like a flower
and when she shouts
all the children bow down with fear.

Dinner time comes
sausage, beans and lovely plums.
Principal Skinner
has found a winner.
Bart sings a song
which didn't last that very long.

Locker doors slamming,
toilet doors jamming.
Lisa's writing a script,
Nelson's book is being ripped
by who, is the mystery.

Samantha Phillips (13)
Whitchurch High School

BLUE

The waves rolled over the deserted sand,
A tear rolled down a lost child's cheek,
A figure sat alone in the desolate silence,
His heart frozen with pain and despair,
Wondering why life is never fair.

Rachel King (12)
Whitchurch High School

PIGS

I'm as round as a football,
Oink! Oink!
I'm as fat as a Christmas pudding,
Oink! Oink!
My back is rough 'cos I've got thick hairs,
Oink! Oink!
I'm pink and loveable,
Oink! Oink!
I roll in mud on a farm, it keeps me cool,
Oink! Oink!
I'll eat raw everything and any leftovers,
Oink! Oink!
I make a lot of noise when I chew,
Oink! Oink!
I trot around my sty all day,
Oink! Oink! Grunt! Grunt!

Kirsty Davies (11)
Whitchurch High School

GUINEA PIG

They're gentle and fast like a cheetah,
Smooth and so soft like silk,
They eat any fruit or vegetable just like us,
Their size is no bigger than your head,
They'll jump up and down like a monkey,
They'll squeak like a gerbil,
They'll natter while eating like a mouse.

Bethan Goodwin (11)
Whitchurch High School

FIREWORKS

No! No! Not again,
That dreadful, terrifying night.

First I smell the fire,
I feel the heat coming from its demonic flames,
A night of terror awaits.

Fear propels me to my bomb shelter,
A moment of stillness, then
Bang! Bang! Boom!
The deafening sound reverberates through my bones.

The sky is falling!
The sky is falling!
Danger, peril, everybody run,
The barrage continues,
I lie in terror,
Waiting to be crushed like a tiny bug.

It's stopped,
We're alive!
Comforters arrive,
I emerge from under the table, go to my bowl,
Extend my canine tongue,
And lap up the soothing water.

Kate Greasley (12)
Whitchurch High School

LIZARD - IGUANA

As deaf as a doornail,
He can't hear.
Warms-up all day, on rocks,
A cold-blooded creature,
He lies in wait,
Soon, a dragonfly
Will meet its fate.
With one swift movement
He darts after it.

As streaky as spaghetti,
He's as green and brown
As a forest
And,
He's light,
He's as slick as a seal,
He's as swift as a swallow.
I admire him,
Greatly.

Michael Willett (11)
Whitchurch High School

MONKEY

Swinging smoothly through the trees,
Chattering to his mate,
His rough hair like a paintbrush,
Brushes through the rainforest
Looking for food for its young.

Ben Franks (11)
Whitchurch High School

HOMEWORK

Homework is hell on Earth.
Every night
you have to fight
to stay up through the night.
Then next day you fall asleep
in lessons here and there.

Then the next night comes,
more and more homework,
can they stop giving us hell
bit by bit.

Next night they go for the kill,
ten times as much,
homework, homework,
when will they stop?
Killing us now, have they lost
the plot or what?

Only five more years to go until
hell is over and school is out.

Lewis John Payne (13)
Whitchurch High School

PIG

You're not very quiet with your wretched oink,
You live in a sty,
You love to roll in mud,
You're pink with a thin layer of fur on your back
and a small tail,
You're killed for pork for us to eat.

Harriet Lacy (11)
Whitchurch High School

A Hamster's Tale

Small and furry,
Soft and squidgy,
His pattering feet
Run around his cage.

Seeds and lettuce,
Cucumber and choc drops,
Up, down, all around
To find his food.

Pale orange
And white,
Fur so soft,
As soft as a duvet which
Covers you at night.

Red eyes,
And pink feet,
With ears
As white as sleet.

Patter, patter,
Squeak, squeak,
Then goes to his nest
And goes to sleep.

Sean McDonnell (12)
Whitchurch High School

A TYPICAL DAY

School!
You know I hate school,
Teachers everywhere,
Acting calm and playing with their hair,
Getting out their pencil case,
And giving us a mean, grotty stare,
As we, the class try to stare it out,
It's thinking of what to do,
Homework, tests and quizzes,
You know that's true!
As it reaches out for the chalk,
A frightened look comes down on our pretty, little faces,
The chalk is out,
It writes,
We copy,
All day long.
We have a break at the end of the day,
And we all know that tomorrow is only round the corner!

Luke Jones (13)
Whitchurch High School

MOUSE

He is small and sly,
He is as white as snow,
His eyes are red like fire,
He squeaks, scratches and sleeps,
He is as soft as soft can be,
And he loves the colour yellow, like cheese.

Kyle Murray (12)
Whitchurch High School

BACK AT SCHOOL ONCE AGAIN

Back at school once again,
with the same old teachers,
with the same old classes,
with the same old people,
with the same old fools.

Back at school once again,
with the old teachers now,
always shouting,
always screaming,
never quiet.

Back at school once again,
with the old classes now,
always dirty,
always rough,
never clean.

Back at school once again,
with the people and the fools,
always quiet,
always shy,
and still they are fools.

Lisa Vaisey (13)
Whitchurch High School

TARANTULA TERROR!

Creeping, crawling fast or slow,
Wherever you are wherever you go,
Furry skin all over its body,
But if it bites you, you will be sorry!

Lee O'Brien (11)
Whitchurch High School

BAT

I am the Hallowe'en animal,
Dracula is my host.
I live in a dark, damp cave,
With no light to guide my way.

I am the winged mouse,
Ebony in colour, my eyes, bright white,
With sharp, round teeth
Which I use to dismember my prey.

I am the upturned mole,
Clinging on for dear life.
Squeaking, squealing, speaking,
My voice, screaming through the air.

Sarah Newington (11)
Whitchurch High School

SPIDER

So many of them, how do you know which one's which?
So furry you want to hold it,
Silent in the house but not in the garden.
Some of them small or medium or *big*.
You can tell they are there because they leave their sign behind.
All of them could get on your nerves,
All of them you want to stamp on, but you can't because it is cruel
Or they live in a beehive.

Lewis Bailey (11)
Whitchurch High School

CATS

As small as a football,
Cats,
Its tongue as sticky as glue on paper,
Cats,
Its paws as soft as a cushion,
Cats,
Its fur as clean as water,
Cats,
Moans with a long miaow,
Cats,
Its tail like a racoon's tail,
Cats,
They sleep in the most strange places.
Cats,
Its food as chewy as a soft Chewit.

Thomas Cox (12)
Whitchurch High School

THE STEEL BEAST

The click of a lever starts it
A gentle purring turns into a loud roaring
It hovers like a dragonfly into the air
It shoots through the sky
Like a beast it cuts through the clouds
As it reaches its goal, it slowly lands
Scattering things beneath it
Then, there is silence.

Lewis Cooke (11)
Whitchurch High School

THE SUN ALWAYS SETS

Not far from here is a beach with sand,
With kids having fun,
Making sandcastles,
Or going fishing,
Their fun will never end;
Until the sun rests its head, among the clouds so grey.

Surfers are showing off their talents,
Catching the waves,
Among others,
Well others have bodyboards and rings,
They're all having fun, happiness is everywhere,
Then everyone goes, the sun has gone,
The beach is nothing more than a cold, strange place.

Victoria Knight (11)
Whitchurch High School

MY OPINION ON TEACHERS

The kids in school
think school's really bad.
My parents think it's good
and so does my dad.
My favourite lesson's games
because we do some sports.
My least favourite lesson is English
because I'm always on report.

Jamie Taylor (13)
Whitchurch High School

I HATE SCHOOL

School, I hate school,
School is just a waste of space.
They could have built a swimming
pool or a cinema,
but no, they built a school.

Oh, and the uniform,
That blue jumper with the
white polo shirt, why couldn't we
have a yellow jumper with a lime
green polo shirt?

Even if it is snowing
and the school is blocked in,
they still manage to find a
way in for us.

I hate school!

Laura Pursey (13)
Whitchurch High School

THE SEASONS

There she was, tiny and weak,
But her strength was increasing day by day.
Lighting up the darkest corners,
Making the dark, dreary mornings bright and gay.

She grew and grew into a fine young lady,
Bringing joy to people's way.
Raising the sun, flowers and people's spirits,
Everyone longs for her to stay.

But alas she went and violence and aggression came,
She stripped the ground and trees of all their wealth.
  She frosted the floor with a crystal white,
Leaving nature shivering with bad health.

  But then all sense of sanity went,
Plants and animals hid in their enclosed holes.
  Destruction continued, it ruled the world,
Gradually, that weak, little girl had lost her soul.

Yasmin Bakerally (13)
Whitchurch High School

THE COMING OF SPRING

Across the soft grey snow field,
A blanket to the land.
Beneath the dark, oppressive storm clouds,
Above the frozen ground.
On the branches of an oak tree, its leaves all long gone,
Alights a tiny robin and bursts forth into song.
The clouds above it part, and bright warm sunshine rains down.
Like a stream of liquid gold in the cold grey panorama of the land.
More birds join the chorus,
And the clouds drift away, on a warm gust of wind from the south.
As the sun appears, the snow begins to melt,
Drip, drip, drip, drip.
The insects leave their winter hidings and return to the world.
A butterfly lands on the branch of a tree,
As it flies away, a tiny bud appears,
Awoken by the birdsong, the animals come forth,
Though the land is still barren, and hard from the frost,
Winter is defeated and spring has come again.

Tom Hedges (14)
Whitchurch High School

I HATE SCHOOL

School, teachers and work,
getting up early
just for school,
in the winter's snow.

Being polite to
the teachers
which makes you
sit in silence.

And doing work
instead of fun.

I hate school.

Aisha Zaman (13)
Whitchurch High School

A WINTER'S MORNING

A winter's morning is very cold,
Gangs of children gang together to keep warm,
The pain of the chilly hands,
The frozen feet.
You blow onto your chilly hands,
The particles in the air as you blow out
Rise up into the deep, dark sky.
That is a December morning.

Gareth Taylor (13)
Whitchurch High School

No Such Thing As School

School is like a prison,
They lock you up all day.
We have to do our schoolwork,
Then they let us out to play.

There are teachers on patrol,
Watching everything we do,
In the yard and on the field,
They're even in the loo.

We have our lunch, then back to class,
It's maths with Mr Poole,
Oh, I wish this world was different
And there was no such thing as school.

Laura Jones (13)
Whitchurch High School

School Caretaker

Every day I sweep that yard,
Morning, day and night,
Spring, summer, autumn, winter.
Those little brats don't know how to keep anything clean,
Haven't they ever heard of bins?
They vandalise toilets, classrooms, tables and chairs,
Writing on walls and tables,
Do you think I care who you love?
If I catch 'em then I'll kill 'em.

Andrew Elford (13)
Whitchurch High School

ANGER

I'm in a cold, dark room, there's someone screaming,
A dark plant is creeping up the dark brown walls,
I try to touch it, but my fingers bleed,
They're so sharp.

The screaming noises are joined by the crash of waves,
The noise is deafening,
I feel cold, very cold,
I touch the plant again,
It's dry and razor-sharp,
It creeps through the gaps in the walls.

The noise is getting louder and the plant closer,
It wraps around me,
The pain is internal,
I let out a shrill scream,
I tear away the plant,
I am angry.

Sam Hartrey (12)
Whitchurch High School

THE OCEAN OF MYSTERY

Below the ocean lies treasures too deep to be found,
Above the ocean lies the mystery of the clouds spinning by,
Beside the ocean stand great giants breaking the waves,
On the bottom of the ocean peacefully lies a jungle full of life,
Between the ocean stand different worlds bursting with life,
Around the ocean swim unknown creatures full of mystery,
On top of the ocean are the monsters never letting the water settle,
Far from the ocean are things like me!

Joseph Emery (12)
Whitchurch High School

I HATE SCHOOL SALAD

I hate school salad,
when we have it in school,
long, stringy stuff,
red stuff, white stuff.

You only get one sausage
on salad days,
the teachers get two.

If I were a rabbit I would like school salad,
or I might prefer a free meal, out on the field,
underneath the roofless sky.

I wonder if rabbits like salad cream?

If I were my guinea pig,
black and cheeky,
I would like the flabby green lettuce
and bits of wet apples,
or I might prefer the garden
and fresh juicy flower shoots.

It's not really the food,
but school that gets me down.

But I do hate salad!

Sally Herbert (13)
Whitchurch High School

CONFUSION

I'm confused,
I'm in a room,
Everything is grey and lifeless,
The room carries on forever into infinity.
The windows and walls are misshapen,
The furniture is angular and strange.
There is no door, I keep walking,
The wall slopes upwards, I keep walking, I can't see the end.
I can't find the door, the answer to my confusion.

I'm confused,
I'm standing in a field of flowers,
The flowers are small,
Their stalks are grey and lifeless,
Their leaves are shrivelled and dead,
They are still.
On top of the stalks sit huge flowers,
They are a bright pink colour with yellow middles.
As I look across the field,
I see the colour drain from the flowers.
Everything is grey.

I'm confused,
I'm walking through a town,
There are fields all around me,
The town is deserted.
The houses are just shells,
Their insides long gone.

Everything is grey and lifeless,
I hear ghostly laughter,
As if a dream,
The laughter goes.
I'm alone,
In a ghostly confusion.

Rachel Davies (12)
Whitchurch High School

AUTUMN

I worm my way into the summer.
I suck the life out of the trees.
Stripping what was once
the great broad leaves.

Look at those smiling children.
Look at them play and sing.
I'll also suck the life out of them,
so they'll do anything but sing.

Now for that happy looking sun.
Now to make it in pain and suffer.
Let's see it die out,
into a little chimney smoker.

This is my favourite part.
This is when the puny human's bow.
They run inside to seek the warmth,
of what I've taken now.

I am autumn!

Scott Finlay (14)
Whitchurch High School

FRIENDS

Friends are jewels
you want to keep forever
and let no one touch them.

Your best friend is winning a
gold medal in the Olympics
and polishing it with great care.

Breaking friends is a puzzle
with one piece missing,
always feeling incomplete.

Enemies are big, black spiders
creeping around in your bed
just waiting for you to feel tired.

A pen friend you've never seen
is being on Blind Date just waiting
to see who's behind the screen.

A friend is stuffing your face full
of chocolate then watching
a soppy film.

Breaking your friendship is
gambling your money away
and not winning any back.

Jenny Dyson (12)
Whitchurch High School

MUSIC

Rain, pounding down on a chilled window,
Thundering, persistent
Getting louder and louder.

A bloodstained knife, tearing bare flesh,
Making vital fluid of life spew from the gash,
Screeching in tribulation.

Filthy litter, circling around a frosty, cobbled,
Empty playground.
Thunder, booming in the overcast, enraged night sky.

Frigid winds gust through a small, lean crack
In a rickety, ancient wall.

A long, venomous rattlesnake,
Slithers ceaselessly in a sandy, deserted
Scorching desert.

Kate Donnelly (12)
Whitchurch High School

THE MOON

T he moon shone bright upon the sky
H igh above the stars
E veryone could fly upon the sky

M oving slowly across the sky
O ver the clouds
O ne day by day going slowly
N ow it's here.

Jody Huntley (11)
Whitchurch High School

FEELINGS

Feelings are like a pomegranate, one minute they are strong and hard,
the next minute it is broken into many pieces.

Feelings are like a newly born baby which is fragile
and can be hurt very easily.

Feelings are like a stream of water gently running down
a hill on a hot summer's day.

Feelings are like a juicy orange when
its burst liquid comes pouring out.

Feelings are like a broken toy being fixed up with glue
making it strong and hard again.

Feelings are like a tower of cards,
one wrong move and it will fall down.

Ben Green (12)
Whitchurch High School

THE DEMISE OF SUMMER

You know when she's struck,
when the trees stand stripped of their glory
and all the dead leaves and the bonfire smoke patrol the skies.
She's just like a witch,
an evil cackling witch who takes delight in dragging
the summer away in chains.
Then she turns the whole country into a mass of gloom and doom.
Who or what is she?
You've guessed it of course - she's autumn.

Christopher Lewis (13)
Whitchurch High School

THE FUTURE

Politicians
Tony Blair, you know the type
Arguing over
What is wrong or right
You need us, they say
'See it our way!'
But then . . .

If all these people are so great
Why aren't they
Preventing all the gloom and hate,
All the diseases and suffering
Before it's too late?
They promise this and they promise that
But really
It's a load of tat.
We'll give you health and education,
They say
But these politicians have had
Their day.

In the future, what we need
Is to get rid of
Our country's greed
Let the world be united
In our happy song
We all know what is right or wrong
So we don't need to argue
All day long.

We're future voices
With something to say
So read our poems
Don't throw them away.

Luke Rogers (12)
Whitchurch High School

A HOUSE

Up above a blue sky,
Full of misty white clouds,
Down below lies Earth,
Full of buildings different shapes and sizes.

At the top of a house lies slates,
Full of nothing but darkness,
Inside are living things,
Full of joy and life.

But the furniture lies still,
Silent, with no life in them at all.

Around the insides of the house are rooms,
Gathered with patterned walls of different colours!

Jessica Thompson (11)
Whitchurch High School

HEAVEN

Above heaven is a world,
of unknown creatures.
In heaven people are riding,
beautiful white horses.
In heaven is a world of love and care.
In heaven is a world of dreams,
coming true.
Under heaven is a world of,
people waiting, waiting for their
dreams to come true.

Stacey Daws (11)
Whitchurch High School

THE OCEAN

I lay on the sand
behind the shimmering seas
below the red-hot sun.
Laying across my rough
but comfortable towel
with its many colours.
Rubbing my soft oily lotion
over and into my
gentle smooth skinned body.
Until I last no longer
in the burning sun.
I go for a swim
in the pale blue water.
Before my eyes
I see a shoal of fish
swimming around my feet,
jet black.
I go further and further
into the water
as I wonder what is beneath me.
I wonder is there another land.
I look beneath the
sparkling waters as I wonder to myself,
could there be another land
or is it just my
imagination going wild?
I will never know for sure
but there is no
harm in looking.
I love the ocean
and will keep coming
back to this beautiful place.

Louise Hoskins (11)
Whitchurch High School

THE OCEAN

Across the water, grey and gloomy,
Above it the sky, black and threatening,
Near, the thunder rumbles, a storm is brewing,
Into the ocean the sky gives up its heavy droplets,
Until their weight marks the sea like the spots of a leopard,
Through the clouds, the lightning strikes,
On the shore, the foaming spray dances on the sand,
Below the water, the swirling sand is carried away,
Before the current dies down and releases its grip,
Over the rocks, the waves roar and spit,
Up and down their rhythm beats,
Beneath them lies a sailor's grave,
In the depths, the ship lies wrecked,
Under the broken ship, the bodies lie in a watery sleep,
Through the night, the storm rages,
Behind the darkness is the light of dawn,
Down the waves die as peace returns,
Far away a lone whale greets the day.

Siân Looker (12)
Whitchurch High School

THE SEA

Under the sea is a mysterious world.
Above the sea, broken up pieces of cotton wool
are glued into a crêpe paper sky.
Far from the sea, a dizzy land is rushing around in daylight.
On the sea, white horses dance.
Way above the sea and land darkness awaits for the sun
to disappear over the horizon.

John Holland (11)
Whitchurch High School

BLACK

It haunts you through the night,
You shiver, you can feel its presence,
The mist is hiding you from the truth,
It is so loud, it is quiet.
You are locked inside a room of ice,
There are sharp pains, you're screaming so loud, no one can hear you,
It is time . . . to make you one of them.
You have been carried to the life of death, dares and no dreams.
You are no longer here,
No one cares for you . . .
And you only come out in the black of Hallowe'en!

Jessica Good (12)
Whitchurch High School

THE SKY

Above the sky lies the dreamworld
In the dreamworld lies heaven
In heaven lies the fast moving grey clouds
Below the sky lies the deep blue sea
In the deep blue sea lies the mysteries of the day
Far from the grey sky lies the lonely green mountains
In the sky lies the miserable grey of the sky.

Stephen De Abreu (11)
Whitchurch High School

AUTUMN

Autumn: like a fiery blaze,
Trying to hold onto the summer's rays.
The wind blowing leaves from far,
Dew covers grass, like a layer of tar.
Scarves come out, heating goes on,
The snow'll be here, won't be long.
Leaves falling from the trees,
Birds fly south, along with the bees.
The hedgehogs and things go off to bed,
For months, silence, not a word said.
Every year autumn comes and goes,
The winter wind comes and away it blows.

Anouska McLean-Smith (13)
Whitchurch High School

THE OCEAN

Upon the ocean white horses dance,
Crashing their hooves on a land of powdered gold.
Far above the ocean, cotton wool buds are studded into a
                                    crêpe paper sky.
Covering a shining pound coin held up by the wind.

Around the ocean and in its depths lies a mystery untold.

Bethan Collins (11)
Whitchurch High School

ICY MORNING

It's dark and cold outside,
But as the words 'Wake up quickly or you'll be late' seep into my head,
Automatically I roll out of bed.
Get dressed quickly, not a second to lose,
Grab my skate bag and on with my shoes.
As we rush past in the frost covered car,
I watch the newsagents opening and eat a cereal bar.

Finally, into the rink I go,
It's empty and chilly and the ice is the colour of snow.
As I step onto the silent ice, the freezing damp air chills me to the bone,
My breath appears like white clouds and I'm all alone.
A ghostly white mist is rising from the surface of the ice
And I circle round slowly one or twice.

Suddenly, the music goes on and I'm skating round fast,
Flying across the hard, wet ice, I'm warm at last.
Down on the ice and sweating I land with a thump,
Soaking and bruised all over but it's worth it when I land that jump!

Lloyd Jones (11)
Whitchurch High School

SPACE

Out in space where spaceships glide and the aliens all hide
The stars twinkle and shine so bright in the darkness of the night
There are lots of planets for you to see, Mars, Jupiter and Mercury
The moon is big just like the sun giving out rays of light and fun
Rockets burst out into space, meteorites floating all over the place
Space is big, tall and wide, there are lots of places where you can hide.

Craig Frederick (11)
Whitchurch High School

AUTUMN

Change is the story of autumn,
skies of blue to skies of grey,
trees of green to seas of leaves,
summer breeze to autumn gale,
scorching sands on beaches to grey and merciless seas,
change is the story of autumn,
autumn is turning a page in a book,
never sure what will be there,
the change is like black or white, night or day,
rich or poor, life or death,
change is the story of autumn.

Benjamin Greasley (14)
Whitchurch High School

BLUE

The mystic, unknown beauty of the morning sea
Dolphins dive through the wild waters
The magical shimmer of the waves in the sun
The sun sets leaving his warm rays on the calm untouched waters
The rippling waves on the surface of the water as the ocean goes to rest.

Sarah Tracey (12)
Whitchurch High School

ORANGE

A colour so bright and lively,
It wakes you up in the morning,
It's like when you open the curtains when it's just gone light,
Or when you turn the light on in a darkened room,
A natural bright light,
Like a light bulb with no cover,
A warm light,
Like lying on the beach with no shade,
Not only a colour,
But a fruit,
A juicy, tasty fruit.

Jenny Leho (12)
Whitchurch High School

BLACK

As black as the night
As cold as stone
It brings depression and loneliness
But never makes a sound
Bats flying round an old church at midnight
Graveyards remembering people's deaths
The crying you hear at funerals
Sadness and evil everywhere.

Bethan Dinnick (12)
Whitchurch High School

BLACK

Silence. That is all you hear.
As the mist hides all your deepest, darkest secrets, the wind haunts you.
Death, with his black cloak and white face,
he picks on victims to join him in hell.
You can't trust anyone, they've all turned against you,
they want to kill you, they want you dead.
As the gothic people spread their evil, you're in a dark room,
you can't see a thing, you can hardly breathe.
The ghosts come out to haunt your dreams with
evil thoughts and evil things.

Katherine Stephen (12)
Whitchurch High School

YELLOW

The fresh lemons lightly swaying
In the morning freshness,
The daffodils growing in the
Blinding sun,
The joy of the freshness in the air,
The night draws near,
Warmth from the fire fills the room.

Lucy Carpenter (12)
Whitchurch High School

WHITE

White is purity.
The doctor who sees your bad leg.
The bride as she accepts her ring.
It is the shower of flags at Wembley
And the nail-biting at Twickenham.
It is the lovely, warm, bubbly, inviting bath,
Just waiting for you to jump in.
White is the still, quiet, silent, peaceful snow.
White is ghosts.

Ben Brown (13)
Whitchurch High School

RED

You can see the flames in his eyes.
His face is red with fury and anger,
His body is still.
He cannot think through the pain,
His friends have left him,
He is lying alone,
His blood is seeping through his uniform.
He has died for his country,
Going, going, gone.

Nicola Williams (12)
Whitchurch High School

AUTUMN

The leaves make a deep red colour
with the pale green, frosty grass peeping
through the fingers of the leaves.
The mist creates a creepy feeling
of someone watching you.
When you walk among the grass
the frost gathers on the front of your shoe.
Leaves stick to your feet and make you feel like a tree.
The wind makes swirling patterns on leaves floating in mid-air.
The snow falls from the sky to your coat
and melts while it's sitting there.

Graham Lasbury (13)
Whitchurch High School

RED

The sun is shining,
You feel the heat.
Liverpool are losing,
They're shouting 'Man U, Man U!'
You get angry,
Tell them you're dangerous.
You feel you could set them on fire,
You shout *stop!*
Or this could be a bloody ending!

Kieran Brown (12)
Whitchurch High School

FAMILIAR SIGHTS AND SMELLS OF SUMMER

The golden sand,
A large stretch of land.
Children playing,
Mothers laying.
Roaring sun,
Fat man's tum.
Water's cold,
Bikinis bold.
Lollipops,
Around their chops.
Familiar smells,
Suncream and gels.
Bronzed girls' hair in curls,
Hunky guys' eyes like skies.
The eternal flame is bright again,
There's nothing better I can say,
About a lovely summer's day.

Emily Hill (13)
Whitchurch High School

GREEN!

You start to go,
Entering the gloomy ghost train,
You start to go green,
You're gonna be sick.
Aliens jumping out from walls,
You envy the people outside,
Whilst the people just about to enter the ghost train
Envy you!

Daryl Bartlett (12)
Whitchurch High School

STORM OF FUTURE FEELINGS

Droplets of crystal clear liquid tumble from the heavens above
Starting off the percussion tune
Light twinkling as it flows
As if it were a river
Now appear the colours of the spectrum
Fading, fading
Disappearing into the everlasting peaceful sky
That never can be ruled by technology
It's all a mystery, how? Where? What? Why?
Mind-boggling questions filter through the mind
How did anything ever begin?
The build up of excitement weaves through you
Waiting to be explored by a unique person
Brave in their own steps
Seeking a new feeling
That tingles inside you
Futuristic domes are the new fashion
Everything's changing, to be up to date would be fate!

Rachel Louise Trusler (11)
Whitchurch High School

RED

Red is the colour of the mind-stealing devil!
The warmth of a glowing fire hitting my face.
The warning of traffic lights to your blood-dripping head!
A wounded soldier lying on the battlefield waiting for his time to end.
Red - the Welsh dragon standing so tall and proud of his country!

Emma Forse (12)
Whitchurch High School

SUMMER

Summer: The gentle breeze
Makes the flowers flow back and forth.
Their brightly coloured petals swaying in the sun.
Singing birds and buzzing bees,
All day long in the trees.
The sight of luscious green grass.
Happy children playing in the sun
Also having great, great fun.
Sun makes me want to feel good,
So as it's summer I think I should.

Daisy Miles (13)
Whitchurch High School

MRS AUTUMN

Mrs Autumn, cold and nippy,
Whirls around her leaves all pretty.
She has long fire-red hair,
Like a magnificent whirl
Of gold, red and orange leaves,
Cascading gracefully down from the trees.
Little children enjoying her presence,
As they trick and treat and get little presents.
The whirl of the Catherine wheel in her eye,
As she falls and waves and says goodbye.

Emily Jane Diamond (13)
Whitchurch High School

OCEAN WORLD

Above the ocean are fluffy light balls of cotton,
Scattered in a blue heaven,
On the ocean are white crashing hands,
Reaching to grab you,
Under the ocean is a magical world of life and mystery,
Colourful to the eye,
Far from the ocean is an abandoned island,
Unknown to man,
On the waves are far away explorers and merchants,
Sailing on huge vessels,
Jutting through the surface of the water are,
Giant sinister boulders, black as coal,
Over the ocean are feathered animals,
Calling, soaring in the air,
Below the ocean are skeletal remains of a wreckage,
Waiting to be discovered,
In the ocean are schools of tropical,
Cold-blooded, gilled creatures floating carefree,
Beyond the ocean is a deck full of emotional beings
Waiting eagerly to welcome their beloved from the sea.

Anita Sivapalan (11)
Whitchurch High School